Crown Copyright Reserved

W.O. CODE NO.

8741

ications/2008

Field Eng_____ _____ ..... Warfare

PAMPHLET No. 7

BOOBY TRAPS

1952

The Naval & Military Press Ltd

in association with

The Imperial War Museum
Department of Printed Books

Published jointly by
The Naval & Military Press Ltd
Unit 10 Ridgewood Industrial Park,
Uckfield, East Sussex,
TN22 5QE England
Tel: +44 (0) 1825 749494
Fax: +44 (0) 1825 765701
www.naval-military-press.com
www.military-genealogy.com
www.militarymaproom.com

and

The Imperial War Museum, London
Department of Printed Books
www.iwm.org.uk

Printed and bound in Great Britain by
CPI Antony Rowe, Chippenham and Eastbourne
In reprinting in facsimile from the original, any imperfections are inevitably reproduced and the quality may fall short of modern type and cartographic standards.

AMENDMENTS

Amendment Number	By whom amended	Date of insertion

DISTRIBUTION

(See Catalogue of War Office Publications, Part II)

RAC, RA, RE, R Sigs, Inf, RAOC and REME .. .. Scale D

Other Arms .. .. Scale A

Attention is drawn to "The Principles and Practice of Good Instruction," Part I which lays down the principles and methods of instruction to be followed by all officers and NCO instructors.

LAYOUT OF FIELD ENGINEERING AND MINE WARFARE PAMPHLETS

Pamphlet No.	Title
1	Basic Field Engineering
2	Field Defences and Obstacles
3	Demolitions
4	Mines—Individual Mechanisms
5	Laying, Recording, Marking and Recovery of Minefields
6	Drills for Breaching of Minefields
7	Booby Traps
8	Assault River Crossings
9	Bomb Reconnaissance and Protection against unexploded bombs.

Field Engineering and Mine Warfare Pamphlets Nos. 7 and 9 both include Part I (All Arms) and Part II (RE and Inf Aslt Pnrs) under one cover.

CONTENTS

	Page
Introduction	1

PART I (All Arms)

Chapter 1.—GENERAL CONSIDERATIONS

Sec
1. The aim and how it can be attained .. 2
2. Booby traps in operations .. 6
3. Responsibilities of all arms .. 7

Chapter 2.—INDIVIDUAL MECHANISMS

4. General .. 10
5. Standard British equipment .. 11
6. Switch No. 4, Pull, Mark 1 .. 13
7. Switch No. 5, Pressure, Mark 1 .. 15
8. Switch No. 6, Release, Mark 1 .. 17
9. Switch No. 9, " L " Delay, Mark 1 .. 19
10. Switch (anti-lift) No. 12, Mark 1 .. 23
11. The Clam .. 26
12. The Limpet, Mark 3 .. 28

Chapter 3.—DETECTION AND CLEARANCE

		Page
13.	Introduction	31
14.	Where to look and what to look for	31
15.	Neutralizing and disarming	34
16.	Organization for searching and clearance	37
17.	General rules	45

PART II (RE and Infantry Assault Pioneers)

Chapter 4.—LAYING AND RECORDING

18.	Planning	45
19.	The design and construction of traps	47
20.	Some typical booby traps	51
21.	Procedure for setting traps	63
22.	Recording	65

APPENDICES

A.	Responsibilities of various arms for booby traps	67
B.	Some notes on training	69
C.	Scales of issue of booby trap equipment	70
D.	Details of packing of booby trap equipment	71
E.	Example of a technical record of a booby trapped area	74

FIGURES

1.	Operation of booby traps	3
2.	Booby trap marking signs	9
3.	Switch No. 4, Pull, Mark 1	14
4.	Switch No. 5, Pressure, Mark 1	16
5.	Switch No. 6, Release, Mark 1	19
6.	Switch No. 9, " L " Delay, Mark 1	21
7.	Switch (anti-lift) No. 12, Mark 1	25
8.	The Clam	26
9.	The Limpet, Mark 3	29
10.	Equipment booby trap sign	39
11.	Mechanism connected to a charge by instantaneous fuze	49
12.	Mechanism connected to a charge by detonating cord	50

		Page
13.	Pull switch connected to an obstacle	51
14.	Pull switch connected to a trip wire	52
15.	Pressure switch set as an anti-personnel device	52
16.	Pressure switch set to operate a railway mine	53
17.	Release switch set under a rifle	54
18.	Release switch concealed in a chest of drawers	55
19.	" L " Delay used in a delayed demolition	55
20.	Uses of anti-personnel mines as booby traps	56
21.	Grenade trap	57
22.	Electric contact traps	58
23.	Pull or release electric contact	59
24.	Electric drawer trap (opening and closing)	66
25.	Flashlight device	60
26.	Electrolytic water butt	61
27.	Shell trap	62
28.	Trip wire attachment for an anti-vehicle trap	63

TRAINING FILMS

(*See* War Office Film Catalogue, Part I)

No.	Showing time (mins)	Title
5112	27	Enemy booby traps, 1942.
827	28	Booby traps and care of ammunition*.

FILM STRIPS

(*See* War Office Film Catalogue, Part III)

No.
FS 782   Principles of Igniters and Basic Mines.

* This is a REME film on recovery of a booby trapped vehicle.

RESTRICTED

FIELD ENGINEERING AND MINE WARFARE

PAMPHLET No. 7
BOOBY TRAPS

INTRODUCTION

Definition

A booby trap is a cunning contrivance, usually of an explosive and lethal nature, designed to catch the unwary enemy; a savage practical joke. It is aimed directly at the reduction of morale and mobility, both of which are vitally important to success in war.

The aims of this pamphlet

This pamphlet has two aims. The first of these is to teach all Arms how to combat the menace of enemy booby traps and to make clear to them their responsibilities in detection and clearance. The second is to teach the Arms concerned (RE and infantry assault pioneers) the principles governing the setting of booby traps and the mechanisms involved.

Layout of the pamphlet

Since the essence of a booby trap is low cunning spiced with variety it is impossible in a short pamphlet to describe in detail all the traps likely to be used by the enemy. A study of our own technique and of the types of mechanisms that we are prepared to use against an enemy will, however, give a good indication of what we may expect from him and will provide a sound basis on which to plan counter-measures.

The pamphlet is, therefore, divided into two parts:

Part I, which describes the principles governing booby trap technique, the types of mechanisms that may be employed (using British mechanisms as examples), and the methods advocated for detection and clearance. This part should be studied by all arms.

Part II, which describes in detail the methods of constructing and setting typical traps, and the rules for recording them. This part is for study by RE and infantry assault pioneers.

Booby traps are a development of the "nuisance mine" technique and many of the rules for mine laying, mine detection and clearance, and of the mechanisms employed, apply also to booby traps. To avoid repetition, reference will be made throughout this pamphlet to the other mine warfare pamphlets, namely No. 4—(Mines—Individual mechanisms), No. 5 (Laying, Recording, Marking and Recovery of Minefields) and No. 6 (Drills for Breaching of Minefields). In addition RE and infantry pioneers should be familiar with Pamphlet No. 3* (Demolitions), which is also referred to.

PART I (All Arms)

CHAPTER 1

GENERAL CONSIDERATIONS

Section 1.—THE AIM AND HOW IT CAN BE ATTAINED

Aim

1. The aim of using booby traps is to create an attitude of uncertainty and suspicion in the enemy's mind, thereby lowering his morale and inducing a degree of caution which slows up his movement. The casualties and damage inflicted are merely means towards this end.

Operation

2. In almost every case booby traps will be operated by one of the following methods :—

- (a) *Pull, ie,* by the movement of some concealed object, such as a thin trip wire, connected to the concealed mechanism (*see* Fig 1 (*a*)).
- (b) *Pressure, ie,* by the direct pressure of a foot, wheel or track on a concealed mechanism (*see* Fig 1 (*b*)).
- (c) *Release, ie,* by the lifting of some apparently harmless object from the concealed mechanism (*see* Fig 1 (*c*)), or by the release of tension in a taut wire (*see* Fig 1 (*d*)).
- (d) *Delay, ie,* by some form of automatic delay mechanism designed to function independently of any human agency.

    The delay may be from a few hours to many days (*see* Fig 1 (*e*)).

3. In the first three types of trap the mechanism may fire the charge immediately or with a delay-action from a few seconds to a few minutes.

---
* Not yet published.

(a) Pull

(b) Pressure

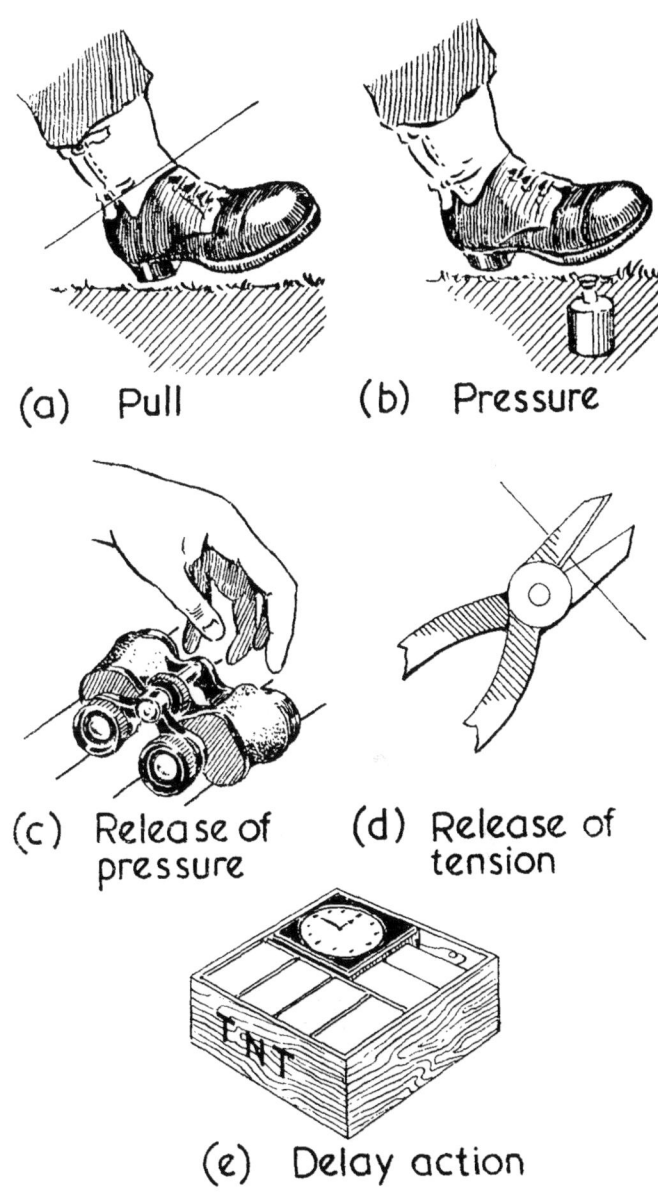

(c) Release of pressure

(d) Release of tension

(e) Delay action

Fig 1.—Operation of booby traps

Principles

4. The essence of a booby trap is low cunning and variety. It will usually take one of the following forms :—

> The baited trap.
>
> The snare.
>
> The double bluff.

or may be a combination of all three.

5. When setting traps the following principles should be observed. Since the enemy will also work on these principles, the understanding of them is important in the detection of traps.

- (a) *Concealment.*—The charges and mechanisms must be concealed or made to resemble some harmless object. The surroundings should be disturbed as little as possible and all signs of preparation should be concealed or removed.

- (b) *Constricted localities.*—The more constricted the site in which a trap is laid the more chance there is of its being sprung and the greater the difficulty of detection and clearance. Any form of defile is therefore a suitable site for booby traps.

- (c) *Concentration of traps.*—Traps should be laid, whenever possible, in considerable concentrations to reduce the chances of finding them all without springing some. Dummies should be used freely.

- (d) *Double bluff.*—An obvious trap may be used to mask a well concealed trap near by.

- (e) *Inconvenience.*—Traps may be operated by the removal of obstacles such as road blocks and demolitions, or of furniture or litter in dug-outs or buildings, particularly if these are suitable for headquarters.

- (f) *Curiosity.*—The handling of souvenirs, pictures, food and drink containers, musical instruments, weapons, etc, may operate a trap.

- (g) *Everyday operations.*—Traps may be operated by opening or closing doors or windows, using telephones or electric light switches etc.

- (h) *Attraction.*—Delay-action or incendiary bombs may attract personnel to a booby trapped site.

- (j) *Alternative methods of firing.*— A trap may be provided with two or more methods of firing.

- (k) *Variety.*—As many different types as possible should be employed in any one locality.

Delay-action charges

6. Although a delay-action charge is not necessarily set off by a " booby ", *ie*, a careless enemy soldier, it nevertheless achieves the same aim by imposing uncertainty and suspicion, and will therefore be considered here. Delay-action charges will usually be aimed to create material damage and should be linked in with the normal demolition plan, but the fact that they go off well behind the lines and some time after the fighting has passed on causes damage to morale as well. The explosion of one or two sows the seeds of suspicion of more, the search for which consumes time and labour and disperses effort.

Trip flares

7. Trip flares are not lethal, but they may be used in the forward areas to give warning of the enemy's approach by night. They operate on the same principles as booby traps and achieve the same purpose. They should be laid on the enemy side of minefields or other obstacles in order to betray attempts by the enemy to remove these obstacles. By lighting up the area they will enable the normal covering fire to be aimed more accurately.

The best results are obtained when flares are set to go off *behind* the enemy thus silhouetting him and facilitating his destruction by our covering fire. Flares going off *between* the enemy and our weapons tend to blind our marksmen and prevent effective killing of enemy, who merely slip away into the background darkness.

8. In rear areas, or in territory where the population is untrustworthy, they can be laid round harbour areas, camps and installations to give warning of the approach of enemy raids or thieves. They can be used alone but will be more effective if sited close to perimeter wire or other obstacles. A disadvantage is that they are frequently set off by dogs or other animals. Repeated false alarms not only waste flares but tend to make sentries careless.

Future developments

9. The principles of booby traps are age-old and are unlikely to alter. The methods of setting traps will vary with the ingenuity and skill of the enemy, but it can be expected that they will study our habits and set their traps accordingly.

10. Mechanisms are much more likely to change with the times. The probable future development of mechanisms and igniters for mines is outlined in Field Engineering and Mine Warfare Pamphlet No. 4, Section 5 and, since booby trap mechanisms are similar to mine igniters, the same ideas may be used. The most likely tendencies are that :—

(a) Traps may be operated by something completely invisible, such as a magnetic field, sounds picked up in a microphone, or a ray actuating a photo-electric cell.

(b) Delay-action charges may be fired by remote control, using radio.

(c) Mechanisms may be made more difficult to neutralize. It can be arranged that the obvious way to neutralize a mechanism is in fact another way to set it off.

Nevertheless it must be remembered that complicated mechanisms are costly and difficult to produce. The use of large numbers of cheap simply made devices will cause more delay and confusion than the threat of a few complicated and outwardly more dangerous ones. A good example of the simple mechanism is the German Schumine with ZZ42 Igniter.

Section 2.—**BOOBY TRAPS IN OPERATIONS**

The withdrawal

1. Booby traps are particularly valuable weapons in a withdrawal to slow up the enemy's advance. They will be laid in much the same way as nuisance mines. Buildings and other accommodation that the enemy may need for shelter and rest, gateways and approaches to attractive harbour areas, diversions round obstacles as well as the obstacles themselves are all likely dividend paying locations. Booby traps are particularly useful for delaying repair-gangs working on damaged roads, railways, airfields, ports and installations.

The defence

2. In addition to their use as nuisance mines on likely lines of approach for men and vehicles, booby traps may be laid in advance of and interspersed in tactical obstacles, *eg*, minefields, wire fences and road blocks, to impede enemy infantry and to prevent detailed reconnaissance and attempted neutralization. They may also be used to give warning of enemy patrols and to deter the enemy from using ground not otherwise covered.

Offensive uses of booby traps

3. During raids in enemy occupied territory delay charges may be used to cause damage and casualties and to create confusion. Normal booby traps may also be left behind to damage and delay the enemy when he counter-attacks to re-occupy the area.

4. When our troops are occupying territory where the inhabitants are hostile, whether in rear areas in wartime or during periods of unrest in peacetime, traps are likely to be used against us in this way.

The problem of detection

5. The detection of enemy booby traps and the reduction of casualties from them is largely a matter of discipline and training. Knowledge of the subject must be combined with keen eyesight and a

suspicious mind. Although the systematic detection and clearance of traps is a task for engineers and specially trained men in the other arms, every soldier must learn to look for the signs of unusual activity which will warn him of traps. He must learn, also, to avoid performing many of the normal actions of life without first of all thinking and looking to make sure that he will not be caught.

Information and intelligence

6. Valuable information about the sites where traps have been laid and the nature of the traps used, can often be obtained from prisoners of war, particularly engineer prisoners. Whilst all prisoners must be evacuated in the normal way, the divisional intelligence staff may be able to return some early for questioning in the suspected area. Local inhabitants, if any, may have valuable information to impart about the activities of the enemy before his withdrawal.

Section 3.—RESPONSIBILITIES OF ALL ARMS

Orders for laying traps

1. Booby traps will only be employed on the orders of divisional commanders and above. **As indiscriminate use is liable to cause many casualties to our own troops the plan must be carefully coordinated by the General Staff.**

Setting

2. Booby traps will only be set by engineers and infantry assault pioneer platoons.

Recording

3. Units setting booby traps are responsible for recording them. The staff are responsible for warning all other units in the neighbourhood. When the area is likely to be re-occupied by friendly troops full details must be recorded, so that traps can be recovered if necessary. These records must be kept by divisional headquarters and handed over to relieving formations.

Detection and clearance

4. Although the responsibility for the detection and clearance of traps rests primarily with the engineers and infantry assault pioneer platoons, field units of other arms are required to maintain detachments trained in the work for the immediate protection of the unit.

5. In the attack all arms must be prepared to accept the danger arising from traps in order that the momentum of the attack may be maintained. Engineers should, whenever possible, accompany the preliminary detailed reconnaissances to discover the existence or otherwise of booby traps and the nature of the traps employed. This information will be given to the troops taking part in the attack.

6. The other arm detachments referred to in paragraph 4 above are required for detection and clearance duties particularly on the first occupation of buildings and harbour areas, including approach roads, as well as during the assault, because it will usually be impracticable to wait until engineers can be spared for the tasks.

7. Even where time and personnel are not available to clear the traps, dangerous sites should be marked for the benefit of other troops that are following. Reports should be sent in giving the area where traps have been found, and any other information available.

8. Where booby traps have been set in large numbers, as may well be the case in an evacuated town, neutralization and removal is the responsibility of the engineers who will carry it out in accordance with priorities laid down by formation commanders.

Marking

9. When booby traps are encountered all arms will mark the area to warn troops that follow. The standard marking sign will be as shown in Fig 2 (*a*). These signs will be issued by Ordnance and carried by field units as part of their war equipment. Signs may also be made up in the field from metal, wood, plastic, composition board or other suitable material. The corners should have small holes for fixing and, if time and material permit, small wire loops should be provided for hanging.

10. The booby trap warning signs shown in Fig 2 (*b*) are now obsolescent. They may be used until stocks are exhausted.

11. Marking signs should, whenever possible, be fixed above ground on wire fences, trees, buildings, or rocks, apex downwards. They can also be stuck into the ground by the point, but this is not a reliable method since they are likely to be obscured by grass and undergrowth and are very easily knocked over.

Trip flares

12. Since trip flares are not lethal they may be laid by any unit at any time ; they need not be recorded.

Training

13. The current training policy on the responsibility of various arms is given in Appendix A, and some notes on training are given in Appendix B.

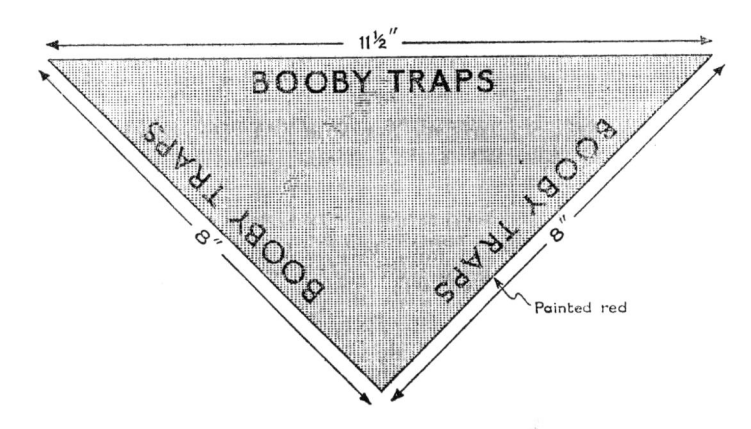

(A) Standard booby trap marking sign

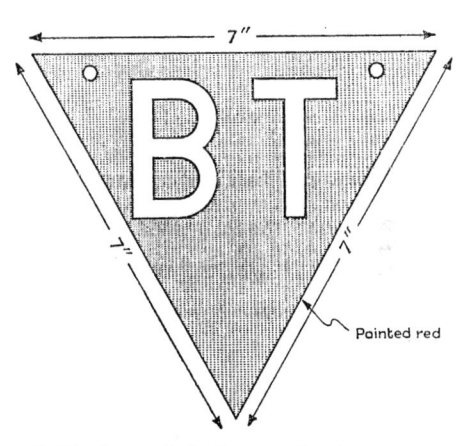

(B) Obsolescent booby trap warning sign

Fig 2.—Booby trap marking signs

CHAPTER 2

INDIVIDUAL MECHANISMS

Section 4.—**GENERAL**

1. Booby trap mechanisms are normally operated externally by one of the following methods :—

(a) By *pull* on a wire.

(b) By *pressure*.

(c) By *release of pressure* or *release of tension* on a wire.

(d) By a *delay-action* device.

2. Internally, the mechanisms work on the same lines as mine igniters. Field Engineering and Mine Warfare Pamphlet No. 4, Chapter 3, describes the eight basic types of igniter ; they are :—

(a) Spring operated, shear pin control.

(b) Spring operated, ball control.

(c) Spring operated, control by pin or plate withdrawal.

(d) Electric contact.

(e) Chemical electric reaction.

(f) Chemical reaction.

(g) Friction.

(h) Inertia.

Spring operated devices are the most common. They consist of a *trigger device* which, when set off, releases a *striker* ; the striker fires a *cap* which initiates a *fuze* ; the fuze is led to a concealed *charge*.

3. *Delay-action* mechanisms can be fired by a variety of methods including :—

(a) Clockwork.

(b) Chemical reaction.

(c) Radio.

(d) Tension on a stretched piece of metal, *eg*, the " L " Delay.

4. The remainder of this chapter is devoted to the standard equipment issued in the British Army. The mechanisms described illustrate each of the basic principles of operation, mentioned in paragraph 1. If these mechanisms are mastered, and if the igniters referred to in paragraph 2 above are well-known, a man should have little difficulty in competing with any new type of mechanism he may meet.

Section 5.—STANDARD BRITISH EQUIPMENT

1. The equipment supplied for the construction of booby traps includes *standard mechanisms, instantaneous fuze,* and *trip wire.* The charges and methods of initiation are made up from standard demolition explosives and accessories.

Mechanisms

2. The *standard mechanisms* are listed below :—

Serial No.	Type	Description	Method of operation	Remarks
1	Pull	Switch No. 4, Pull, Mark 1.	Pull of 6-8 lb.	
2	Push	Switch No. 5, Pressure, Mark 1.	Pressure of 21 to 60 lb.	40-55 lb when load applied to extension rod.
3	Release	Switch No. 6, Release, Mark 1.	Release of pressure.	Minimum safe pressure 7 lb.
4	Delay	Switch No. 9 "L" Delay, Mark 1.	Slow stretching and breaking of lead rod.	1 hr to 28 days delay.
5	Anti-lift	Switch (anti-lift) No. 12, Mark 1.	Release of pressure (especially for use with anti-tank mines)	Not normally issued to units. **Only to be used on Army Commanders authority.**

All these mechanisms have a standard *cap* and *cap holder* and a standard *fuze adapter.* Extra caps and cap holders, in boxes of one hundred, are provided for use with them. The mechanisms (except the " L " Delay) can be used up to five times in training provided that a new cap and cap holder is used each time. They are described in detail in Sections 6 to 10 inclusive.

Instantaneous fuze

3. *Fuze, Instantaneous, Mark* 4, is a burning fuze encased in an orange covered fabric. It burns at not less than 90 feet per second but will not detonate. It can be lighted by a standard booby trap mechanism or a percussion igniter and will fire a detonator. It is

used to connect standard mechanisms to explosive charges, or it can be used in training to simulate safely the explosion of a booby trap. It is important to remember that the US Army uses an orange coloured safety fuze which burns at two feet per minute. Great care must be taken to ensure that these two fuzes are not confused.

Trip wire

4. *Trip wire* (·032 in) is the standard issue (1951). It is strong enough to trip up a 14-stone man running at full speed ; it can therefore be used to give warning of the approach of the enemy as well as for booby traps. If standard wire is not available, the wire selected should be tempered and have a dark finish, to make it difficult to see.

Trap wire

5. Wire used for connecting booby trap mechanisms to movable objects is known as *trap wire*. There is no standard issue ; wire selected should be as thin and invisible as possible, provided that it is strong enough to operate the mechanism.

6. A combined trip and trap wire may be introduced in the near future.

Miscellaneous equipment

7. Other standard equipment that may be used for booby traps includes *anti-personnel mines, percussion igniters, Clams, Limpets,* and *trip flares.*

8. *Anti-personnel mines.*—An anti-personnel mine is a ready made booby trap. Details of the British anti-personnel and shrapnel mines will be found in Field Engineering and Mine Warfare Pamphlet No. 4. The anti-personnel mines No. 5 and No. 6 can be used as pressure operated traps ; the shrapnel mine is set off by a pull on a trip wire.

9. *The Igniter, Safety Fuze, Percussion, Mark* 3, is a standard demolition accessory, and is described in Field Engineering and Mine Warfare Pamphlet No. 3*. It can be used as a pull mechanism by attaching a trip wire to the safety pin.

10. *Clams* and *Limpets* are ready made demolition charges for use in raids and sabotage operations ; they are normally initiated by delay-action mechanisms. They are fully described in Sections 11 and 12 below.

11. *The British Infantry Trip Flare, Mark* 1 is described in Field Engineering and Mine Warfare Pamphlet No. 4.

---

*Not yet published

Scales of issue and packing

12. Booby trap mechanisms and ancilliary equipment form part of the war equipment of engineer field units and of assault pioneer platoons of infantry battalions. They are also carried in the explosives lorries of divisional RASC colums. Details of the scales of issue are given in Appendix C. Details of the packing of standard equipments are given in Appendix D.

Section 6.—SWITCH No. 4, PULL, MARK 1

Description

1. This is a pull mechanism of the spring operated type, control being by pin withdrawal. It can be used with movable objects such as doors, windows, furniture, or souvenirs, or with trip wires.

2. The mechanism consists of the following parts (*see* Fig 3) :—

   (a) A *brass case* with two *fixing eyes*.

   (b) A standard *adapter assembly*, consisting of a *spring mount* and body holding the *percussion cap*, screwed into one end of the brass case.

   (c) The *striker*, actuated by a *spring*, and held in position by the *U-shaped clip* which grips the rounded end of the striker.

   (d) The *safety pin*, which passes through a hole in the end of the striker and through slits in the case.

3. The overall dimensions of the mechanism including the spring adapter are $3\frac{1}{4}$ inches by $\frac{7}{16}$ inch diameter, and its weight is $1\frac{1}{4}$ ounces.

Operation

4. A pull of six to eight pounds on a trip wire attached to the U-shaped clip will withdraw the clip and thereby release the striker.

5. *To arm:*—

   (a) Attach a trip wire to the U-shaped clip.

   (b) Tension the trip wire until the safety pin lies about half way along the slot in the body.

   (c) Remove the safety pin.

6. *To neutralize* :—

   (a) Insert a spare safety pin, a nail, or a piece of strong wire in the safety pin hole.

   (b) Trace and cut the trip wire.

7. *To reset* (for use in training) :—

   (a) Unscrew the fuze adapter.

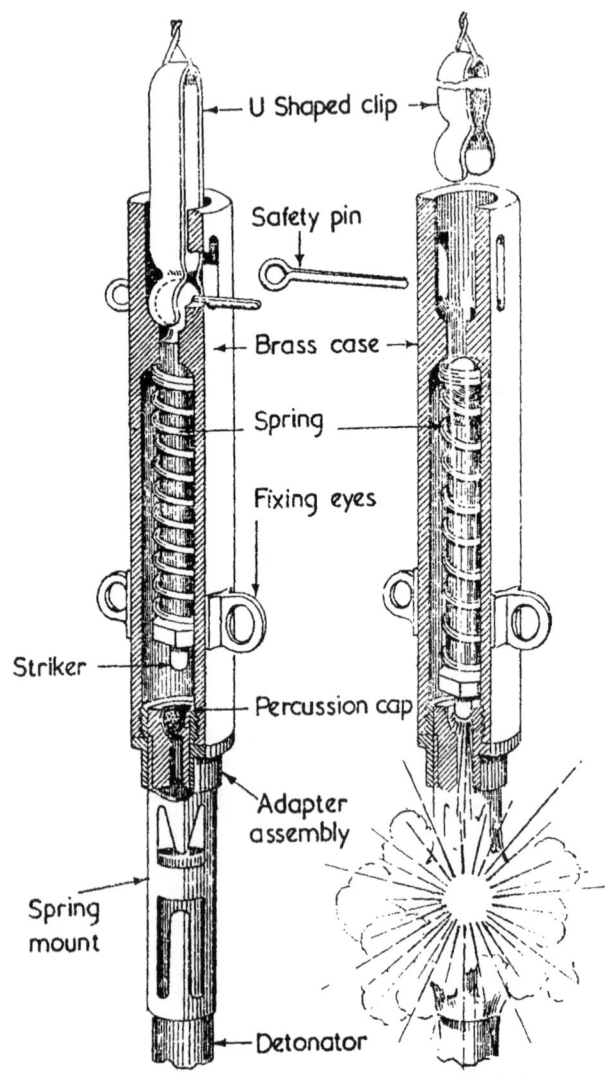

Fig 3.—Switch No. 4, Pull, Mark 1 (*actual size*)

(b) Push back the striker as far as it will go with a pencil or rectifier.

(c) Twist the striker rod until the safety pin hole is in line with the two slots in the body, using a safety pin as a tommy bar.

(d) Fit the U-shaped clip over the ball end of striker rod and allow the striker to come forward about $\frac{1}{4}$ inch.

(e) Insert the safety pin.

(f) Screw in a new adapter with percussion cap.

Section 7.—SWITCH No. 5, PRESSURE, MARK 1

Description

1. This is a pressure mechanism of the spring operated type, control being by plate withdrawal. It can be used under floor boards, staircases, furniture, and under stones or boards concealed in roads or paths. A special extension makes it suitable for use under railway lines.

2. The mechanism consists of the following parts (*see* Fig 4):—

(a) The *body* enclosed in the *case* and covered by the *lid* hinged at one end. There are two small holes in the bottom of the case to facilitate fixing.

(b) The double *sear* with two lips engaging in the *detent* in the *striker stem*.

(c) The *striker* operated by a *spring*.

(d) A standard *adapter assembly* is screwed into the case.

(e) A *safety pin* (a two-inch by $\frac{1}{16}$-inch split pin), which fits through the body, under the sear, and through a hole in the striker stem. To this pin is attached a short length of tarred string.

(f) An *extension socket* which screws into a central hole in the lid and which takes an adjustable *extension rod*.

The weight of the switch is approximately $4\frac{1}{2}$ ounces, and the overall dimensions (including fuze adapter) $3\frac{3}{4}$ inches by $1\frac{1}{4}$ inches wide by $\frac{3}{4}$ inch high.

Operation

3. (a) A small depression of the lid of the mechanism depresses the sear on its spring. This releases the striker which flies forward under the pressure of its spring and strikes the percussion cap.

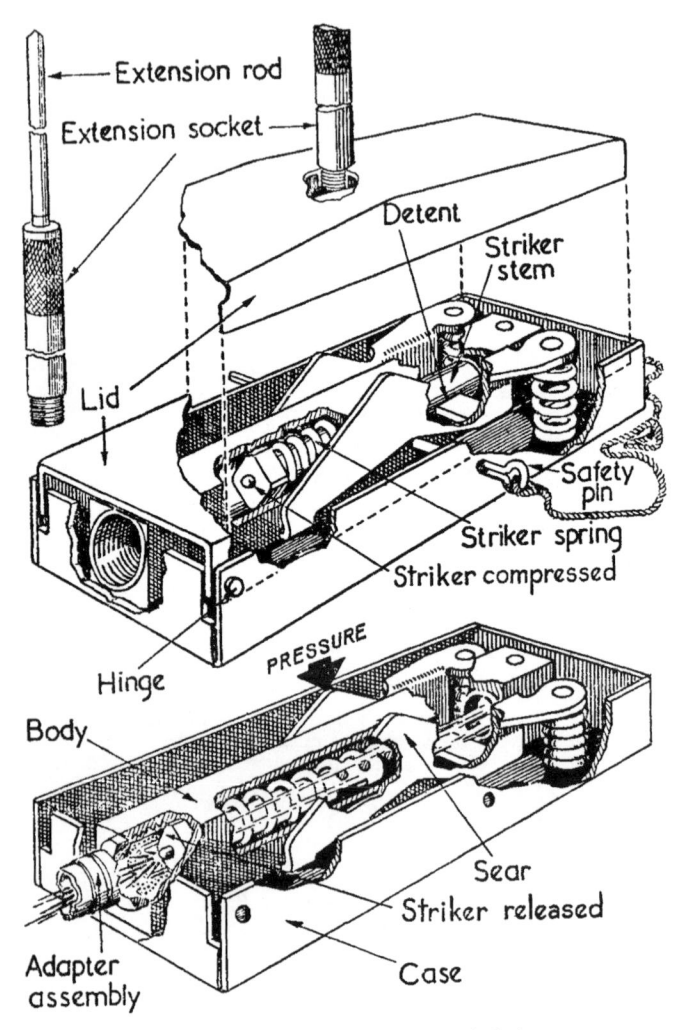

Fig 4.—Switch No. 5, Pressure, Mark 1

(b) The pressure required to operate the mechanism varies with the position on the lid on which it acts. At the end furthest from the hinges a pressure of about 21 lb is needed ; at the extension socket from 50 to 60 lb.

4. *To arm* :—

   (a) When used for booby traps :—

   (i) Set up the mechanism in close contact with the object that is to conceal and operate it. Take out the cap and cap holder but do not connect the fuze.

   (ii) Withdraw the safety pin.

   (iii) Ensure that the mechanism does not go off under the weight of the object alone but that it does go off under the weight of a man.

   (iv) Reset the mechanism and insert the safety pin, replace the cap and connect the fuze to the fuze adapter.

   (v) Withdraw the safety pin again. If the mechanism is inaccessible withdraw the safety pin with a wire or cord.

   (b) When used for railway mines :—

   (i) Firmly bed the mechanism in the ballast of the track midway between the sleepers and under a rail, ensuring that the extension rod is about $\frac{1}{4}$ inch beneath the rail.

   (ii) Unscrew the rod until contact is made with the rail.

   (iii) Withdraw the safety pin.

Note.—If excessive pressure is applied when setting up, the safety pin will not withdraw easily. Do not try to force it.

5. *To neutralize*.—Insert a spare safety pin, a nail, or a piece of strong wire in the safety pin hole.

6. *To reset* (*for use in training or when testing*) :—

   (a) Unscrew the fuze adapter.

   (b) Insert an extension rod or pencil, keeping a good pressure on the switch.

   (c) As soon as the striker is home release the pressure on the switch and the sear will then re-engage the detent and hold the striker.

   (d) Insert the safety pin.

   (e) Screw in a new adapter with percussion cap.

Section 8.—SWITCH No. 6, RELEASE, MARK 1

Description

1. This is a release mechanism of the spring operated type, control being by plate withdrawal. It is so shaped that it can be in-

serted into a narrow opening, as under a drawer or behind a door. The limit of weight which the mechanism will resist is that required to crush it. It can therefore be used under a heavy weight such as a packing case. It can also be used under any objects which are likely to be lifted, such as boxes, souvenirs, etc.

2. This mechanism consists of the following parts (*see* Fig 5) :—
  (a) The *case* of the switch, on which fits the *lid* hinged at one end.
  (b) The *striker* fits in the case and is held in position by the *safety pin*.
  (c) When the lid is seated down on the case, a hinged *sear* engages in a *detent* in the *striker stem* and holds the striker back against the *spring*.
  (d) A stop pin limits the movement of the sear in an upward direction.
  (e) The case is threaded at one end to take a standard *adapter assembly* and *percussion cap*.

The overall dimensions including fuze adapter, are 4½ inches by ⅝ inch by $\frac{9}{16}$ inch, and its weight is 3½ ounces.

Operation

3. (a) Before the mechanism is fixed, the striker is held in position by the safety pin only. In this state the pin requires considerable force to remove it.
  (b) When a weight of about 3½ pounds or more is brought on the lid, the sear forces back the striker and unlocks the safety pin which can then be withdrawn easily. A 7-pound weight is the minimum that should be used for safety.
  (c) When the weight on the lid is lifted the sear is pushed away by the detent, and the striker is then driven forward by its spring.

4. *To arm* :—
  (a) Place the mechanism under a weight of at least 7 pounds.
  (b) Withdraw the safety pin. If the pin will not withdraw easily do not force it. If the mechanism is inaccessible withdraw the pin with a wire or cord.

5. *To neutralize* :—
  (a) Insert a spare safety pin, a nail, or a piece of strong wire in the safety pin hole.
  (b) If the mechanism is inaccessible it may be necessary to cut the fuze instead. Care must be taken that the mechanism is not disturbed while this is being done.

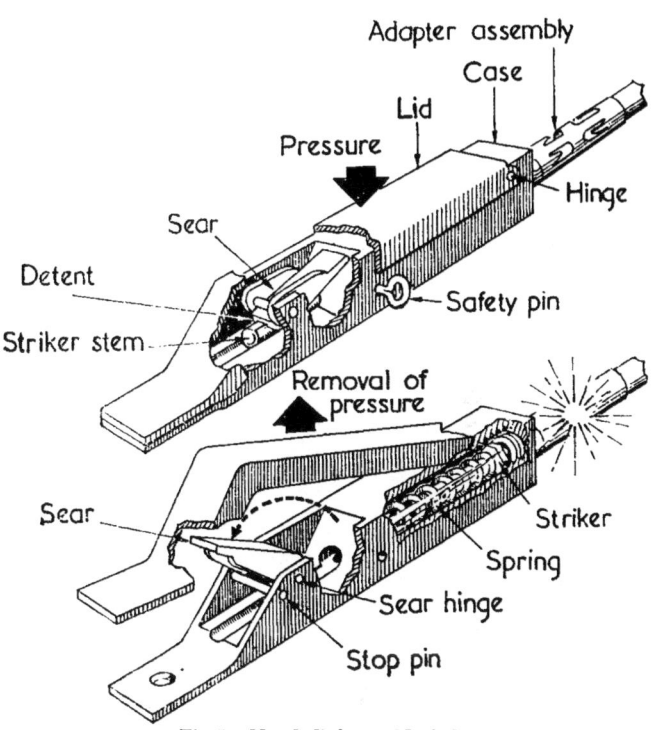

Fig 5.—No. 6, Release, Mark 1

6. *To reset (for use in training)* :—

(a) Unscrew the adapter and withdraw the striker and spring.
(b) Open the lid and throw the sear over until it rests on the stop pin.
(c) Re-insert the spring and striker, detent uppermost.
(d) With a pencil or rod force the striker back until the safety pin can be inserted.
(e) Throw the sear forward and close the lid of the switch.
(f) Screw in a new adapter with a percussion cap.

Section 9.—SWITCH No. 9, " L " DELAY, MARK 1

Description

1. This is a delay-action mechanism working on the principle that Tellurium lead under tension stretches uniformly with time and will break eventually. The mechanism can be used for firing a charge or

lighting an incendiary. It can be used in raids behind the enemy lines, by partisans and guerillas, or for delayed demolitions in a withdrawal.

2. The device is 4 inches long by ⅜ inch diameter, and will operate in any position. In any one device the delay period cannot be adjusted, but separate devices are provided to give different periods.

3. Standard switches are available for the following periods :—

1, 6, 12, and 24 hours ; 3, 7, 14, and 28 days.

These times only hold good when the average temperature is 65°F. At higher temperatures the delay period is reduced ; at lower temperatures it is increased.

4. Each device carries a tab stating the timing at 65°F. A correction table (*see* paragraph 10) gives the timing at other temperatures. Whilst the degree of accuracy claimed by the manufacturers is only + 30 per cent, experience has shown that errors greater than 10 per cent are unusual.

5. Should no standard delay be suitable for a particular operation any special timing from one hour to one month can be supplied, provided that the temperature at which the device is to work is given.

Operation (*see* Fig 6)

6. A *spring-loaded striker pin* is anchored to the outer tube by the *lead element*. When the element breaks it releases the striker pin, which is forced down by the spring so that its point fires a *cap*. The cap fires a *detonator* or ignites a *fuze*.

7. Normally a *starting pin* removes all load from the element. This pin passes through holes in the outer tube which register with a clearance hole in the head of the striker. A turned back portion of the pin then re-enters the tube to come hard up against the underside of the head, preventing any movement. A spring *safety clip* keeps the starting pin in place and, in some switches, a small nut is found as well.

8. When the starting pin is removed the load is transferred to the element and the device is set in action. If the pin is difficult to move it is probable that the element is faulty ; the switch should be replaced and destroyed. Instructions for the inspection of switches before arming are given in paragraph 13 below.

Note.—(*a*) Two fuzes should be provided for each important charge to guard against the risk of failure.
(*b*) In damp locations the joint between the "L" Delay and safety fuze must be waterproofed with adhesive tape. The tape should cover the pressure relief holes.

Method of issue

9. The "L" Delay fuzes are packed in boxes of 10. Those issued for operational purposes contain 10 assorted fuzes as follows :—

Times of delay	Assortment "A" (quantities)	Assortment "B" (quantities)
1 hour	2	3
6 hours	2	2
12 hours	2	2
24 hours	2	1
3 days	2	1
7 days	–	1
Totals	10	10

The boxes issued for training contain 10 fuzes, each of 1 hour delay.

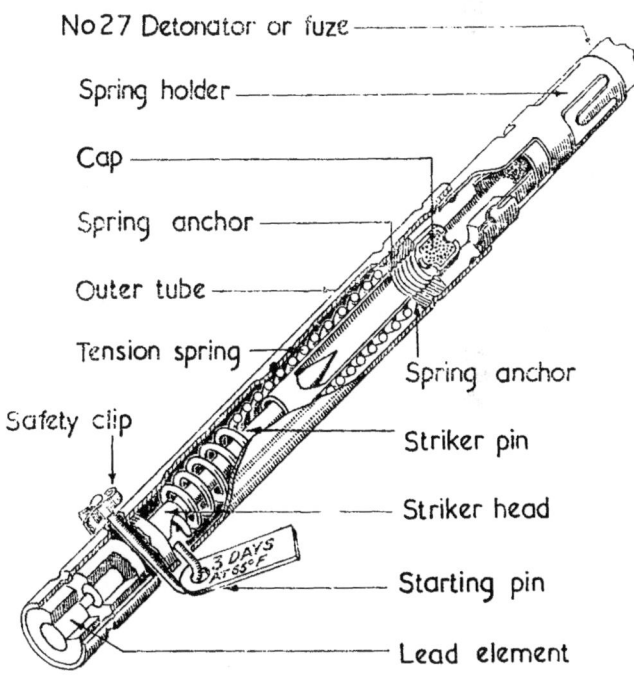

Fig 6.—Switch No. 9, "L" Delay, Mark 1

Selection of an " L " Delay

10. To select the correct mechanism for an operation first estimate the temperature at which it will have to work, and decide what time of delay is actually required. The table below should then be consulted.

Correction factors for " L " Delays at various temperatures

°F	Hours				Days			
105	¼	1½	3	6	½	2	4	7
95	½	2	4½	8	1	2½	5	10
85	½	3	6	12	1½	4	7	14
75	¾	4	8	17	2	5	10	20
65	1	6	12	24	3	7	14	28
55	1½	8	17	33	4	10	19	39
45	2	11	23	46	6	13	27	54
35	3	16	32	64	8	19	38	75

11. On the appropriate temperature line choose the nearest timing to the one decided upon, then find in that column the underlined figure. This figure gives the labelling of the " L " Delay which should be used.

12. As an example, say an 8-hour delay is required where the average temperature is 95°F. Look along the 95°F line and find the eight-hour figure. The underlined figure in the same column is 24 so the " L " Delay to use will be labelled " 24 hours at 65°F ". Allowing for a ten per cent variation one way or the other it will fire somewhere in the period between seven and nine hours.

Inspection

13. Before arming an " L " Delay it is vital to inspect it to make sure that it is safe to use. The following points should be observed :—
  (a) Look through the starting pin hole from the side opposite to the head.
  (b) Apart from the pin the hole should be perfectly clear all the way through.
  (c) If the lead element has started to creep it will be seen to have partially blocked the hole.
  (d) If the lead element has started to creep across the hole it means that the " L " Delay is dangerous and must be destroyed. The pin must not be touched.

To arm

14. After inspection, arm the device as follows :—
    (a) Remove the small spring clip on the starting pin.
    (b) If the pin head is held by a nut, remove this nut by unscrewing it.
    (c) Pull out the starting pin by its tab.

Safety precautions

15. Always inspect the " L " Delays before arming.

16. These units cannot be dismantled and examined, and it is dangerous to interfere with them once the starting pin has been removed as there is a risk of premature firing if subjected to shock.

Neutralization

17. If it is necessary to disarm a charge that is set with an " L " Delay the fuze must be cut. Great care must be taken not to jolt the delay. There is no way to neutralize the " L " Delay itself and it must be very carefully removed and destroyed.

Section 10.—SWITCH (ANTI-LIFT) No. 12, MARK 1

Special notes

1. The switch (anti-lift) No. 12, Mark 1 is provided for use under British anti-tank mines. Although it can also be used under grenades No. 75, or in booby traps, such uses are not recommended.

2. This switch will not normally be issued to units. It will be kept in theatre stocks ; only Army Commanders may authorize its use. When authorized, engineers only will lay and record the devices.

3. The description and operation are inserted in Part I in order to give all Arms an illustration of a typical anti-lifting device that they may meet in enemy laid mines and traps.

4. The switch will not normally be lifted. In exceptional cases this may be done but only by specially trained, skilled engineer personnel. In minefields being lifted, mines incorporating the device should normally be destroyed *in situ*.

Description

5. The switch is composed essentially of two parts (*see* Fig 7), the *explosive* container and the *main housing tube*. The explosive container is a shallow tapered drum containing 4 ounces of RDX/TNT and has a tube running through the centre which contains the *detonator unit* and spring-loaded *striker*.

6. In transit the detonator unit is replaced by a *wooden transit plug*. The striker has a *hollow spindle*, *split* at the *head* so that it can be collapsed. When collapsed it will pass through a small *bush* at the

bottom of the *extension tube*. When the switch is cocked, however, this spindle is held open by the *retaining rod*, which is contained with the *lift spring* in the bottom of the main housing tube. The explosive container and extension tube are held down in the main housing tube by a *safety pin*, which runs through an eyelet on the base of the container and a turned over portion of the *flange* at the top of the main housing tube. As soon as this pin is removed the explosive container will rise under the influence of the lift spring. A weight of approximately 2½ pounds is required to hold the container down.

Operation

7. The switch is placed in position with a weight of over 2½ pounds on top of the container. When this weight is removed the container and the attached tube will move upwards under the influence of the lift spring. After moving approximately ¾ inch the striker spindle will be lifted clear of the retaining rod. The split head will then collapse and slip through the bush and the striker will then fly upwards under the influence of the striker spring and fire the 4-gr detonator. This will in turn detonate the CE pellets and the main charge.

Setting

8. The switch may be set under an anti-tank mine or under any other object weighing over 2½ pounds. The following drill is recommended for use with mines :—

 (a) Prepare a hole for the mine with an accurately level bottom and dig a narrow channel off to one side. The length of the channel should be equal to the length of the arming wire (attached to the safety pin) plus one foot. The bed of the channel must be on the same level as the bed of the mine hole.
 (b) Push the spike on the end of the housing tube into the ground until the safety pin is level with the bed of the mine hole. The transit pin should have been removed previously, but the wooden transit plug should be left in position.
 (c) Lay the arming wire along the trench in prolongation of the axis of the safety pin.
 (d) Remove the wooden transit plug and insert the detonator unit.
 (e) Lay the mine so that its weight rests on the head of the switch and ensure that the projecting rim on the bottom of the mine is not holding the weight of the mine off the switch.
 (f) Fill in round the mine and half way along the trench.
 (g) Arm and camouflage the mine, then camouflage the filled part of the trench.

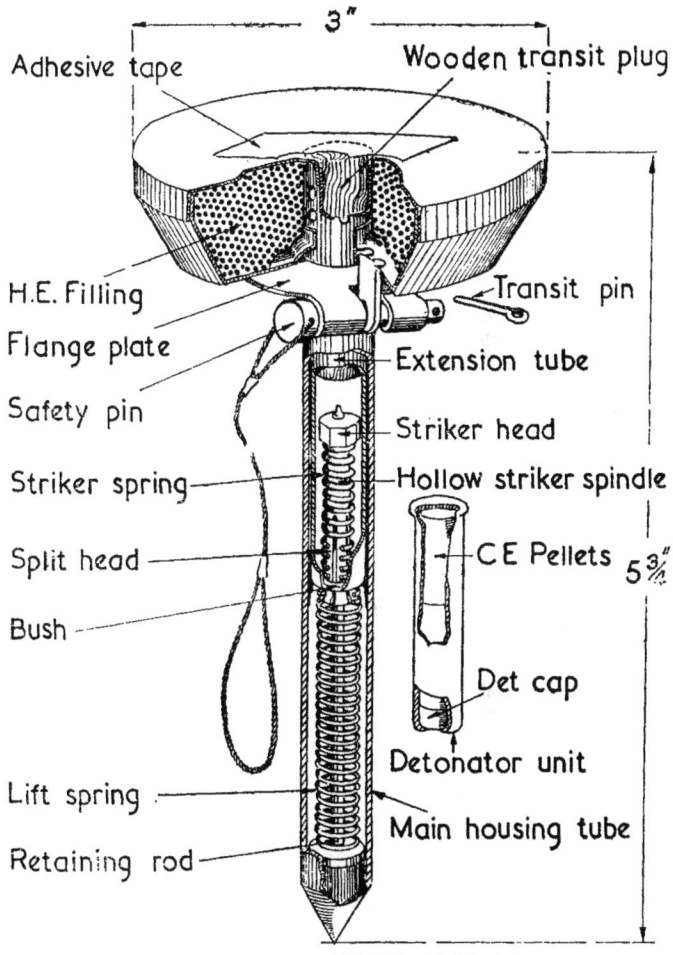

Fig 7.—Switch (anti-lift) No. 12, Mark 1

(*h*) Arm the switch by withdrawing the safety pin, steadily and gently, with the arming wire. Great care must be taken to ensure that the pull on the arming wire is directly along the bed of the trench and not upwards.

(*j*) Remove the arming wire and the pin and fill in the remainder of the trench and camouflage it.

9. Great care must be taken to ensure that the pull on the arming wire is in continuation with the axis of the safety pin. If, however, the safety pin does not pull free on arming the switch, ON NO ACCOUNT will any attempt be made to investigate or to put this right. ON NO ACCOUNT will any force be exerted on the arming wire. If the safety pin is stuck, undue force will result in tilting the switch so causing premature firing. The rest of the channel must be filled in and the switch must be considered armed. The camouflaging of the mine itself should be done before the anti-lifting switch is armed in case it should be moved in the process.

Neutralization

10. Mines incorporating this device should not be lifted but should be destroyed *in situ*.

11. The switch may be allowed to operate (minus detonator and CE pellets) in training, and can be put together again. Care must be exercised to ensure that the striker does not fly out and cause injury

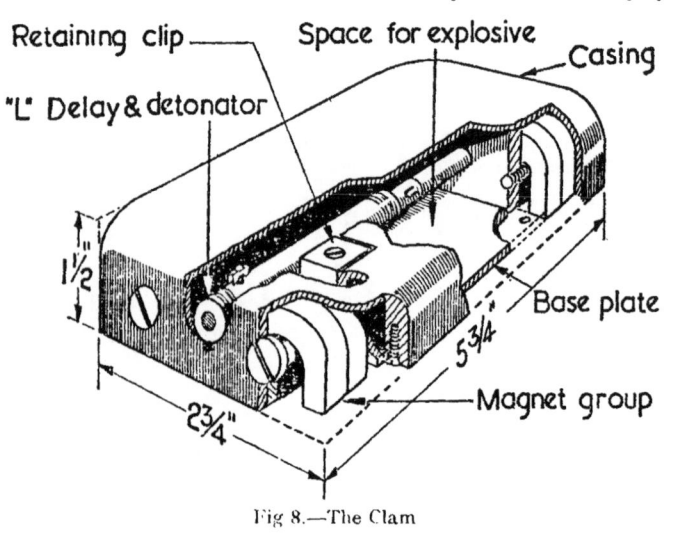

Fig 8.—The Clam

Section 11.—THE CLAM

General description

1. The Clam (*see* Fig 8) is a small time bomb with a magnetic base by which it can be attached instantly to any flat iron or steel surface. Sufficient high explosive (8 ounces) is carried to hole a 25-mm plate, fracture an engine cylinder block or to bend a railway line.

2. The Clam is shaped in the form of an oblong moulded box, with rounded corners, measuring 5¾ inches by 2¾ inches by 1½ inches. At each end of this box is a magnet compartment, the two magnets being loosely indented in the base so that they can get a grip on an uneven surface. The centre compartment of the box is filled with high explosive and closed with a flat lid held in place by four screws. This lid should not be removed.

3. A standard " *L* " *Delay*, with a *No. 27 detonator* attached, serves as the initiator. It slips into a groove at the top of the body and is gripped by a small clip. A wooden plug takes the place of the delay unit until the clam is armed.

Method of issue

4. Clams are a special store, to be demanded only for special tasks. They are issued in wooden boxes of 50. A full box weighs 102¼ pounds and measures 22 inches by 15¼ inches by 9 inches. The standard explosive filling is TNT/Tetryl 55/54 which is proof against small arms fire. If necessary to fulfil some special requirement Clams can be supplied empty or with an alternative filling.

5. On opening the box it will be found that the units are packed in pairs with the magnet faces together. To break a pair, slide the clams away from each other endways, not sideways, until they come apart. On no account hold them even momentarily so that the magnets repel each other; if this occurs the magnets will suffer a permanent loss in pulling power.

6. Each clam is complete and ready for use except for the addition of an " L " Delay and No. 27 detonator. Boxes of " L " Delays containing an A or B assortment are usually issued with clams (*see* Section 9).

To arm

7. (*a*) Select a suitable " L " Delay (*see* Section 9).

   (*b*) Insert a No. 27 detonator into the spring holder of the " L " Delay.

(*c*) Slip out the wooden plug and slide the "L" Delay into its place, making sure that it is pushed right home.

Filling

8. If unfilled clams are supplied the most convenient explosive to use with them is plastic. Remove the cover plate by taking out the four countersunk screws and slide out the wooden plug. 4-ounce sticks of the explosive should now be kneaded together and packed into the cavity.

9. As the magnets are retained in position by the lid, they may accidentally drop out when it is removed. They must be replaced the proper way round in their compartments before the lid can be replaced. Then drive the four screws well home and re-insert the wooden plug, forcing it right home so that a cavity is formed in the explosive for the detonator.

Installation

10. Before approaching the target, remove the safety clip of the "L" Delay. The starting pin should be left in place until the clam is in position, and then pulled out. Hold the clam securely whilst pulling it out. Once this pin has been removed the delay can fire prematurely if subjected to the shock of being dropped on the floor.

11. The clam can be applied to any flat iron or steel surface. When using it on a vehicle remember that it may be subjected to severe jolting; if attached to a smooth vertical plate it might, under such conditions, gradually slide down.

Section 12.—THE LIMPET, MARK 3

General description

1. The Limpet (*see* Figure 9) is a larger edition of the clam designed to be fitted instantly to any iron or steel target—such as an oil tank or the side of a ship. It will function either on land or under water, and carries a charge of $3\frac{1}{2}$ pounds of high explosive—enough to hole a 60-mm plate. Exceptionally powerful segmental magnets give it a good grip even on a lumpy surface.

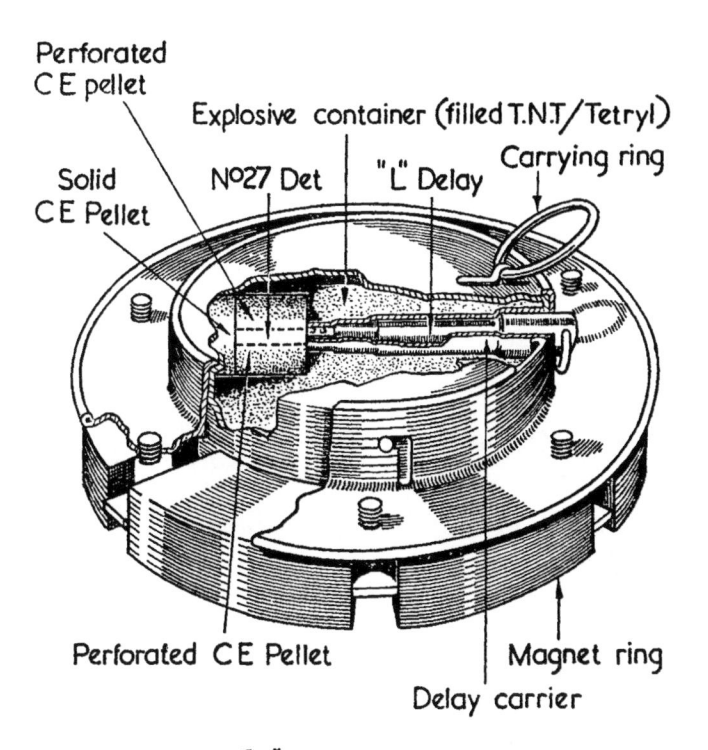

Perforated C E pellet
Explosive container (filled T.N.T/Tetryl)
Solid C E Pellet
Nº 27 Det
"L" Delay
Carrying ring
Perforated C E Pellet
Delay carrier
Magnet ring

Diameter = $9\tfrac{5}{16}''$
Height = $2\tfrac{1}{16}''$

Fig 9.—The Limpet, Mark 3

2. The *explosive container* is a separate unit which can be detached from the *magnet ring* so that the device can be used without magnets if desired. It is filled with a high explosive which is proof against small arms fire and weighs 4¼ pounds. The magnet ring weighs 5¼ pounds bringing the total weight of the device to 9½ pounds. The weight in water is 6½ pounds.

3. A standard " *L* " *Delay with No. 27 detonator* serves as the initiator. It is fitted into a special *carrier* which gives a watertight joint when inserted in the magazine.

4. Each limpet is complete and ready for use, except for the addition of an " L " Delay and No. 27 detonator. The standard " L " Delay boxes are usually issued with limpets (*see* Section 9).

Preparation for use

5. Select a suitable " L " Delay, as described in Section 9, and insert a No. 27 detonator into its spring holder.

6. Remove the delay carrier from the Limpet by pulling it out of the magazine. Inside this carrier will be found a wooden former plug. Discard it, and slide the " L " Delay into its place. The rubber ring on the carrier tube should be positioned on the engraved red line.

7. The delay carrier can now be replaced, but it will be found that the starting pin and tag of the delay prevent it from being pushed past a certain point. In this condition the limpet is quite safe. Arming is completed by removing the safety clip from the starting pin of the delay, pulling out this starting pin, and then pushing the delay carrier right home.

8. Even when the device is being used on land it is advisable—although not essential—to push home the carrier after removing the pin. For underwater work it is absolutely essential to carry out this operation before the device is immersed. Otherwise there will be a risk of water putting the initiator out of action.

Installation

9. If for use on a vessel, the limpet should be attached, if possible, 4 or 5 feet below the waterline and preferably amidships. It is best to avoid placing it on the bows or stern where it is liable to meet severe wash should the vessel proceed at any speed. Actual tests have indicated that, even in these unfavourable positions, given a reasonably good surface, it will remain in place up to at least 16 knots.

10. If a cord is attached to the *carrying ring* of the magazine, the device can be dangled below water until it comes into contact with its target, when it will quickly attach itself.

11. If the Limpet, Mark 3, is to be used as a normal time-delay demolition charge, it is a simple matter to dispense with the magnet ring. After removing the delay carrier, it will be found that the magazine is fixed with a bayonet catch into the magnet ring and can be detached by giving it a slight turn in the anti-clockwise direction. The delay carrier is then replaced in the magazine.

12. Should only a short delay be required, the limpet can be set off with a No. 27 detonator at the end of a length of safety fuze. If instantaneous detonation is required the device can be fired electrically using a No. 33 electric detonator. Care must always be taken to see that the detonator is pushed well home in the magazine tube. By stuffing this tube with plasticine or clay a fairly good waterproof joint can be made.

CHAPTER 3

DETECTION AND CLEARANCE

Section 13.—INTRODUCTION

1. Chapter 1 of this pamphlet has dealt with the general principles governing the use of booby traps in operations, and the responsibility of the various arms for the detection, clearance, laying and recording of traps. As a lead-up to the solution of the problems of detection and clearance Chapter 2 described the operation and uses of the standard British mechanisms, the experience of the 1939-45 war having shown that the equipment used by all armies was basically the same, differing only in details of construction.

2. This chapter deals with the problems of detection and subsequent clearance of enemy booby traps. Although, as already stated, the responsibility for this rests primarily on the engineers and infantry assault pioneers, field units of other arms are required to maintain detachments trained in these duties. This chapter must therefore be studied by *all Arms*.

3. Before discussing the procedures used for detection and clearance it is necessary to answer two questions. The first of these is, " How can a trap be found ? " and the second is, " How can a trap be made safe ? " Section 14 is therefore devoted to a study of possible enemy methods and of clues which may guide the searcher ; while Section 15 deals with methods of neutralizing and disarming various types of traps. Section 16 then deals in detail with suggested procedures for searching and clearance of traps under varying conditions. Section 17 concludes the chapter and Part I of the pamphlet with a series of safety rules for those dealing with booby traps.

Section 14.—WHERE TO LOOK AND WHAT TO LOOK FOR

1. *Look everywhere*.—The essence of good booby trapping being low cunning and variety, there can be no guarantee that any particular square yard of ground, any single room or any piece of jettisoned equipment in territory recently abandoned by the enemy is free of traps. Even international conventions for the conduct of war may be disregarded by an unscrupulous and desperate enemy, and instances have been recorded of booby traps linked with the dead and wounded. Continual vigilance is vital. It must become second nature.

2. *The more likely places*.—Since there is a limit to the resources of time labour and material that the enemy can devote to booby trapping, it is probable that his main effort will be made in places where the greatest number of casualties is likely to result. The principles governing the selection of sites are detailed in Section 1, to which reference should be made.

Sites and objects to suspect

3. When following up a retreating enemy the following sites should be suspect :—

   (a) *Roads and railways.*—Cuttings, embankments, blind bends, bridges, culverts, obstacles and the area round them, wooded stretches, junctions, cross roads.

   (b) *Open country.*—Woods, trees, posts, gates, paths, hedges, obstacles, stores dumps, fire trenches, shelters and other field defences.

   (c) *Buildings and dugouts.*—Steps, floors, doors, windows, cupboards, passages, furniture, fireplaces, water taps, lavatories, supplies, light switches, floor coverings, pictures, documents.

   (d) *Undemolished installations* and *vulnerable points* such as power stations, coal mines, important bridges etc.

4. In rear areas or in occupied territories where unrest is rife, the following places are often mined or trapped :—

   (a) *Railways.*—The track may be mined with a pressure switch, or else destroyed by a charge fired electrically by guerillas who lie hidden until the train comes by. The most likely places are in woods or other defiles or on bridges.

   (b) *Sites of incidents.*—After serious outrages such as explosions in buildings or vulnerable points, or after raids on camps and installations, all approaches to the scene may be mined or trapped. In addition anything left behind after the raid must be suspected.

   (c) *Illegal arms caches.*—Arms caches and other illegal stores may be trapped to cause casualties to searchers.

Clues

5. The following may indicate the presence of a trap :—

   (a) Movable and apparently undamaged equipment and vehicles, food and drink and their containers, kitchen utensils, or anything likely to make a souvenir.

   (b) Disturbed ground and small subsidences, especially after rain.

   (c) Spoil, explosive wrappings, saw-dust, and nose caps from shells.

   (d) Footprints in soil, foreign to the nature of the ground, *eg,* chalk marks, where no chalk exists on the surface.

   (e) Traces of camouflage, withered vegetation, etc, indicating some attempt at concealment.

   (f) Breaks in the continuity of vegetation, dust, paint-work, timbering, etc.

- (g) The presence of pegs, nails, electric leads, pieces of wire or cord for no apparent reason.
- (h) Marks on trees, on paths, on the ground or on walls of buildings without an obvious reason. Such marks may have been used by enemy reconnaissance parties to indicate sites selected for traps.
- (j) Minor obstructions of all kinds on roads, in trench systems and in buildings. Heaps of dead leaves, litter etc.
- (k) Irregular foot or wheeled traffic tracks for whose presence there is no apparent reason.
- (l) Loose floor boards, signs of digging, recently re-laid brickwork in cellars, or hollow sounding walls should be all suspected. These may well be the only clues to the presence of deeply buried delay-action charges.

There is no end to such a list. A soldier must, by training and experience learn " **mine sense.**" This " sense " will warn him of traps more surely than any list.

Particular problems

6. The following extract from a report on German traps in Florence in 1944 illustrates the problem of concentration of traps :—

" Rubble from the demolitions was trapped with shrapnel and anti-tank mines, some being set as anti-personnel booby traps with pull switches and trip wires. The presence of other metal in the rubble added to the difficulty of detection with either mine detectors or prodders . . ."

" Booby traps were skilfully laid, many types of explosives and mines being used. Trip wires were cleverly concealed by leaves and the use of coloured wire out of doors, and by scattered clothing, documents, etc, indoors. Many shutters, door handles, floors and pieces of furniture were efficiently trapped . . ."

7. *Bluff*.—Large numbers of dummies may often be found. Provided that only one or two traps are put amongst them, caution is imposed on our troops and the enemy's aim is achieved. At the same time troops become careless after finding large numbers of dummies ; when this happens they are more likely to be caught by the cleverly placed live trap.

8. *Alternative methods of firing*.—Charges may be set off by more than one mechanism, or a mechanism may operate on more than one principle, *eg* :—

- (a) Pressure mechanisms may be concealed under a trip wire in order to catch a man tracing along it to find its end.

- (b) A mechanism may work on the *pull-release* system. This type is usually attached to a taut trip wire. It will go off when the wire is pulled, but if the wire is cut the release of tension will also spring it.
- (c) A *pressure-release* mechanism is a pressure mechanism that will also go off when the pressure is released. If one is placed under a floor board or railway line it will go off when pulled out by a searcher, unless it is first made safe.

Section 15.—NEUTRALIZING AND DISARMING

1. Neutralizing is the process of rendering a mechanism inoperative and safe to handle; disarming is the process of removing the mechanism or igniter from the main charge, thus rendering it harmless.

2. There are three ways of getting rid of a trap :—
- (a) By pulling with a cable and grapnel, *ie*, by setting it off intentionally from a safe distance or by dragging the mechanism clear of the charge (*pulling*).
- (b) By destroying it with a small explosive charge (*destruction in situ*). This method is for use with particularly dangerous traps where method (a) cannot be applied.
- (c) By neutralizing and disarming by hand (*the "hand" method*)

These methods are dealt with in detail in the following paragraphs.

Pulling and destruction in situ

3. These methods should be used whenever the resultant damage can be accepted. They are the safest methods for the clearance parties and are particularly applicable out of doors. In applying the described procedure below extreme care must be taken in each case not to disturb the mechanism when placing the grapnel and pulling cable or demolition charge.

4. *A trip wire* will be dealt with by placing the hook of the grapnel as close as possible to but not touching the wire. If it is necessary to provide a support for the grapnel (as in the case of a high wire) be sure that the support is stable and will not collapse when the pull is exerted.

5. *Pull and release mechanisms* will be dealt with by pulling away the objects that conceal and operate them.

6. *Pressure mechanisms* will be removed by pulling them out from beneath the objects that conceal and operate them.

7. *Charges* can also be removed by pulling; they should be treated carefully since separate mechanisms may be concealed within or beneath them.

8. If it is impossible to attach a grapnel to a booby trap without disturbing the mechanisms, it should be destroyed *in situ* by a small charge of explosive detonated in contact with the main charge. If the main charge cannot be got at safely the explosive should be placed carefully alongside the mechanism. The damage resulting from the explosion may be reduced to a minimum by use of sandbags or similar protection.

Neutralizing and disarming by hand

9. Since pulling and destruction *in situ* cause damage to surroundings there will be times when it is necessary to neutralize and disarm traps by hand. This method should only be used by arms other than engineers or infantry assault pioneers when they are quite certain that the trap they are dealing with is simple in nature and familiar to them in principle. The method is most likely to be used during the clearance of a building (*see* Section 16), but if any of the traps are particularly dangerous to handle, being awkwardly situated, cunningly designed or already partly sprung, hand methods should not be employed ; if the damage resulting from pulling or destruction *in situ* is likely to be excessive the area should be marked off and reported to the engineers.

10. If for any reason the damage that may result from the explosion of the charge is not acceptable, as for instance when large charges are found in important buildings, close to valuable machinery or near an important bridge, the commander ordering clearance may rule that all traps are to be neutralized by hand no matter how dangerous and complicated the mechanisms may be. Unless the mechanisms found are straightforward and well known, clearance parties of arms other than engineers or infantry assault pioneers should not attempt to neutralize or remove them but should mark them and report them to the engineers.

11. The following sequence for neutralizing is given as a guide only ; the exact sequence for any particular trap will depend on the nature of the mechanism and its accessibility.

  (a) Without disturbing the mechanism, carefully examine the complete set-up and check for alternative means of firing.
  (b) *Slack* trip wire may be cut immediately, but both ends should be traced to discover the nature and location of the traps involved.
  (c) *Taut* trip wires must be traced to the main mechanism. They must not be cut.

Note.—When tracing along trip wires, whether taut or slack, take care not to disturb them, and make sure that pressure switches are not set beneath them.

(d) Without disturbing the mechanism cut the fuze or leads between the mechanism and the main charge. (Treat *taut* leads with suspicion : they may function with a release switch in the main charge). This action corresponds to the first stage of disarming. Whenever it can be performed it is the quickest way to make booby traps harmless with the least likelihood of damage or danger.

(e) Replace the safety device (or equivalent nail, wire, etc) in each apparent mechanism.

(f) Remove the mechanism to a safe place.

Delay-action mechanisms

12. Simple delay-action mechanisms can be handled gently except at the appointed time. They should be withdrawn carefully from the charge or detached from it by cutting the fuze. Delay-action charges with complicated fuzes should be marked and reported to the engineers. Whenever delay-action mechanisms are discovered anti-handling devices and other booby traps should be suspected.

Choice of method

13. It will be seen from the foregoing paragraphs that when a booby trap is discovered there are four courses open. These are :—

(a) To pull it with a grapnel.

(b) To destroy it by hand-placed charge of explosive.

(c) To neutralize it and disarm it by hand.

(d) To mark it off and report it.

14. The choice of method will depend upon the following factors :—

(a) The degree of importance of the site.

(b) The design, position and state of the trap.

(c) The size of the charge, its placing and the damage that may result from the explosion.

(d) The state of training and experience of the clearance party. The table below summarizes the instructions given in this Section. It must be taken as a guide only. Commanders ordering clearance must appreciate the situation locally and must lay down clearly the degree of damage that is acceptable and the amount of risk that is justifiable, *ie*, whether dangerous traps are to be pulled or exploded, neutralized by hand, or merely marked off and left.

CLEARANCE OF BOOBY TRAPS

Site	Simple traps Category* "B"	Simple traps Category* "C"	Dangerous traps Category* "B"	Dangerous traps Category* "C"	Remarks
In the open	Pull or explode	Pull or explode	Pull or explode	Pull or explode	Damage acceptable
In ordinary buildings	Hand	Hand	Pull explode or mark and report	Pull or explode; hand if ordered	Damage to be kept to a minimum
Near specially vulnerable targets	Hand if ordered	Hand	Mark and report	Hand if ordered	All damage to be avoided. Depends on size and placing of charges

* The definition and responsibilities of the various categories of personnel are given in Appendix A.

15. The methods given above are those that will normally be used during wartime in operational areas. In non-operational areas or in disturbed areas in peace time the risk to the clearance parties will not be so justifiable and except on extremely important sites it will be normal to accept the damage resulting from pulling or explosion. Standing orders should lay down the local policy.

Section 16.—ORGANIZATION FOR SEARCHING AND CLEARANCE

General

1. The procedure for searching and clearance will be considered under three headings :—

(a) In houses and buildings.

(b) In the open.

(c) Other situations.

2. It must be realized that it is not only difficult but also unwise to lay down exact rules for booby trap clearance. Every trap may be different and must be considered on its merits using the principles

given in this pamphlet. Furthermore, should the enemy realize that we have adopted a standard method, he would soon devise means of trapping of such a nature that our standard methods would only lead us into danger. The following instructions must therefore be taken as a guide only.

Preparations

3. Before starting on the job a suitable party must be organized and equipped. Clear orders must be issued covering the degree of damage and risk that is to be accepted. Unless they have special orders clearance parties will *not* attempt to neutralize complicated and dangerous traps, (*see* Section 15).

4. All or some of the following equipment and tools may be needed, depending upon the methods to be adopted :—

   (a) *Mine detectors and prodders.*—Mine detectors will rarely be of much use indoors because traps will often be concealed near metal objects. Out of doors they are of assistance except on railway lines or near bridges or other steel structures. Prodders will be useful out of doors, for detecting hard buried objects, and for revealing places where hard ground has recently been disturbed.

   (b) *Lengths of steel wire.*—Lengths of 14 SWG steel wire should be used to feel for trip wires. It is essential to use a steel wire since softer material without temper will not reveal the difference between trip wires and twigs or grass. Too weak a feeler will not detect a trip wire at all. A bare forearm also makes a sensitive feeler but it is not so good at distinguishing trip wire from grass or twigs ; in attempting to discover the difference the trap may be sprung.

   (c) *Grapnels and cable.*—A 50-yard length of whipcord or signal wire, fitted with a grapnel or hook at one end, for use as a pulling cable.

   (d) *Chalk.*—Chalk is needed to mark routes and progress inside buildings.

   (e) *Eyeshields.*—Some form of eyeshield should be worn by all men working on detection and clearance as a protection against small explosions otherwise harmless. Pending the introduction of a standard pattern, eyeshields should be improvised in the field from old respirators.

   (f) *Marking signs.*—Standard marking signs, as shown in Fig 2 (a) on page 9, will be used to mark areas where traps have been found but not cleared. At present standard signs as shown in Fig 10, are issued to engineer field units as part of Set B Minefield Marking Stores (*see* Field Engineering and Mine Warfare Pamphlet No. 6).

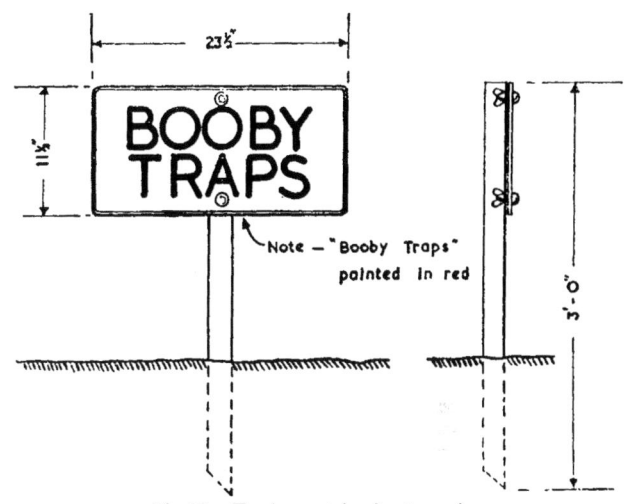

Fig 10.—Equipment booby trap sign

These signs will continue in use until stocks are exhausted. In addition to the signs issued by Ordnance the engineers in a formation will usually manufacture and issue signs for use in the formation area.

(g) *A ladder.*—A ladder may be needed to get into a house by an upper window or through the roof, in the event of ground floor entrances being trapped.

(h) *Tracing tape.*—Tracing tape is needed to mark safe routes, especially out of doors. It may also be used to mark off areas that have not yet been cleared.

If booby traps are to be neutralized by hand, the following additional items will be needed :—

(j) Pliers, scissors and jack-knives for cutting wires and fuzes etc.

(k) A torch and small hand mirror, for use when mechanisms are in awkward places.

(l) A collection of safety pins, nails and pieces of wire for use as such. Pieces of wire and nails should be thick enough to fill pin holes without forcing, and strong enough not to bend when in use. Half-inch nails and 15 or 16 SWG wire are usually the best sizes.

Searching and clearance in houses and buildings

5. Houses and buildings offer excellent opportunities for booby trapping and, because of the possibility of a concentration of traps in the restricted area, the task of searching and clearance needs particularly careful organization. Since houses are so often needed by all arms and services, particularly in cold climates, damage must be avoided as far as possible, and the procedure given below should be clearly understood by the specialist detachments in field units of all arms as well as by engineers and infantry assault pioneers.

6. The size of party to be employed will depend upon the size and nature of the building to be searched and the number of men available. The maximum party should be two men per room. Only one floor of a building and only half the number of rooms on that floor should be searched at one time. Parties should not work in adjacent rooms.

7. *Exterior reconnaissance and entrance to the building.*—Before approaching the building, the garden and path will first be checked for mines and traps. The commander of the party and one soldier will then reconnoitre all doors and windows and select their point of entry. Doors should be avoided unless they can be seen to be safe or are open. Doorsteps must also be suspected. Windows must be carefully searched before opening, and if there is any doubt the glass should be broken and entry gained without moving the sash. If all doors and windows are suspect a hole in the roof should be used the route to the selected point will then be marked with tape.

8. *Interior reconnaissance and establishment of a control point.*— After entering the building the commander and one soldier will reconnoitre and establish a control point, keeping a careful look out for booby traps as they go. The route from the point of entry to the control point will be marked on the floor with chalk.

9. The commander will then find out which rooms can be entered from the control point, *ie*, those which have open doors. He will then return to the point of entry to fetch the clearance party. The soldier will clear any traps near the control point.

10. *Organization for clearance.*—The commander will decide which rooms are to be searched first and will detail men for these rooms. He will tell them the point of entry to use, whether by door or window, and make sure that they all know the location of the control point.

11. *Sequence of searching a room.*—The men will search their respective rooms in the following order :—

   (a) Floors and furniture.
   (b) Walls, including doors, windows, fireplaces, built-in cupboards, etc.
   (c) Fittings (including light switches, etc), and pictures.

12. *Neutralization.*—As each trap is discovered it will be neutralized by hand in the way described in Section 15, paragraph 11.

Those that are considered by the men themselves to be too difficult to neutralize will be clearly marked and left.

13. When the men have finished a room they will mark the door with chalk saying either:—

"ROOM OK" *or*
"BOOBY TRAPS"

and will report to the commander saying :—

(a) That no traps were found *or*

(b) details of traps found and neutralized *and*

(c) traps found but not neutralized.

They will bring with them all disarmed charges and mechanisms and dump them near the control point.

14. The commander will then detail the next room to be searched and, if necessary, a new control point to be brought into use.

15. When all searching and neutraliztion is complete the parties will return to the control point. They will pick up all charges and mechanisms collected there and leave the building.

16. The commander with, if necessary, one other man will then examine all traps that were reported to him as being too dangerous to neutralize. He will then decide whether or not they are to be neutralized and if not, whether they are to be removed by pulling or destroyed *in situ*, or marked and reported to the engineers. This decision will depend upon the situation and the orders that he has been given.

17. *Procedure for pulling*.—To prepare for pulling first place the grapnel near the trap but not touching it. Then run the cable out through a convenient door or window. A suitable covered point should now be chosen for the puller; all the other men should move away to a safe distance. The grapnel should next be connected to the trap by the most suitable method, as outlined in Section 15, paras 3 to 7.

After the cable has been pulled all men should remain under cover for at least ten seconds in case the charge is fired by a short delay fuze.

18. *Procedure for destruction in situ*.—The minimum party will be used for placing charges. Before the fuze is lit the remainder of the party will take cover. The party will remain under cover for at least ten seconds after the bang in case there is a secondary charge connected by a short delay fuze.

19. *Marking*.—When the task is finally completed the commander will mark the building with a sign saying either :—

(a) "NO TRAPS", *or*

(b) "TRAPS CLEARED".

together with his unit sign, using the standard signboards in use in his formation. If he has had to leave any traps for the engineers he will mark the house clearly with a sign saying, " BOOBY TRAPS " (*see* paragraph 4 (*f*) above) and will report the full details to his superior officer.

20. General points to be observed :—

(*a*) Before a door is opened, both sides must be examined. If necessary this will be done by cutting out a panel. The outsides of closed doors can be inspected and cleared by the commander or his assistant. The search parties who entered by the window can then be informed.

(*b*) All floors, furniture, walls, fittings, doors, etc, searched and proved or rendered safe will be marked " OK " in chalk. Both sides of a door will be so marked, and in addition when a room has been cleared the outside of the door will be marked " ROOM OK ", together with the initials of the man who cleared it. Doors must not be marked until both sides have been searched and the door opened.

(*c*) After a maximum of 10 minutes searching every man must rest for a few minutes.

(*d*) A break of 20 minutes must be observed in every 1½ hours.

(*e*) On no account must any man continue searching if anything is likely to disturb his concentration, such as the approach of another person or a conversation overheard. He must wait until the interruption ceases.

Searching and clearance in the open

21. The clearance of traps on routes or in large areas in the open will usually be combined with mine clearance, and will be carried out by the engineers, or by assault pioneer platoons in infantry battalions. The methods to be employed and the equipment needed are described in Field Engineering and Mine Warfare Pamphlet No. 6.

22. Small areas in the open such as approaches to buildings, sites for HQ's, wreckage from demolitions, obstacles, and the ground around them, are likely to contain anti-personnel mines mixed with other traps. In such places it will not always be possible to use deliberate mine clearance drills and procedure will have to be varied to suit the circumstances. Nevertheless, the procedure given above for use in buildings provides a good guide, and whatever the circumstances may be, the following are essential :—

(*a*) *Reconnaissance.*—This must be carried out first to establish whether or not traps are there and if so their locations.

(*b*) *Establishment of a control point.*—From the control point safe routes should be marked out to the traps by tracing tape.

(c) *Organization of the party.*—Individuals or pairs should be sent to each trap, but they must not bunch together.

(d) *Neutralization.*—Explosions in the open are far less likely to cause serious damage so the normal methods of disposal will be pulling or destruction by a small hand placed charge. When traps are being pulled or exploded all men should be kept under cover at a safe distance.

(e) *Marking.*—When traps are destroyed or cleared, the extent of the cleared area should be marked with signs and tracing tape. In addition the limits of any area that still contains traps should be clearly marked with tracing tape and the signs described in paragraph 4 (f) above.

Other situations when searching and clearance may be necessary

Some examples of other situations are given in the succeeding paragraphs.

23. *Booby trapped obstacles.*—Booby traps are frequently laid together with other obstacles such as craters, demolitions or road blocks. Their purpose is to catch the parties sent to remove these obstacles and to slow down the work of reopening the route. For example the lip of a crater may be sown with pressure devices or anti-personnel mines, as may the abutments and approaches to a demolished bridge. Anti-tank mines or other anti-vehicle devices may be laid to catch bulldozers or armoured equipment sent to work on the obstacle. Movable blocks such as trees, wreckage from demolished bridges, wire or immobilised vehicles may be attached to pull mechanisms. Live or dummy mines scattered across the road may conceal trap mechanisms or other anti-handling devices. In addition the obvious diversion round any obstacle is usually mined or trapped.

24. All obstacles should therefore be searched and cleared of traps before being removed. The obvious diversion must always be checked before it is used. The simplest way to deal with a movable obstacle is to attach a strong cable to it and pull it with an armoured vehicle. All booby traps attached to it will then be exploded, but mines and anti-personnel devices in the road may still remain dangerous. The men attaching the cable must take care that they are not caught by trip wires or pressure devices as they approach.

25. *Railway lines.*—These are favourite targets in occupied areas where subversive forces are active. Ordinary plate-laying gangs can usually detect a disturbance to the track, and in most cases the mechanism can be seen where it comes into contact with the rail. The special clearance parties will then only be needed to neutralize the mechanism, or to destroy it *in situ*, depending on their orders. Routine searching may be ordered daily or special searches may be ordered before important trains. Unskilled men may be used as

covering parties and should be able to find or scare away hidden saboteurs lying up to fire the charge by electrical methods as the train arrives. Electrical cables leading to their hideouts may give them away, but searchers should be careful that the ground under the cable itself is not trapped.

26. One of the simplest ways of proving a railway track is to push an empty wagon ahead of each train, or in front of the first train each day. This method will not prevent damage to the track nor will it be of any use if the charges are fired electrically by hidden raiders.

27. *Delay-action devices.*—These are difficult to discover because they may be deeply buried and therefore perfectly hidden. They will often be attached to very large charges. Very often the earliest indications that the enemy is using them will be the explosion of the first one. After this a search will have to be made of the likely sites such as important buildings to be used as HQ, valuable installations or bridges left undemolished. The clues to their whereabouts were described in Section 14. It is difficult for men without knowledge of building construction to appreciate where the charges are likely to be so, whenever possible, the task of searching for them should be given to engineers. If devices are found they can be neutralized by any of the methods given in Section 15, depending upon the circumstances and orders given but, since delay action charges are often designed to cause material damage, hand neutralization will frequently be necessary.

28. *Sabotage.*—The methods used by hostile parties to bring charges complete with delay mechanisms into our camp and installations are likely to be ingenious and desperate. They can only be forestalled by a thorough check of identity coupled with a search of their vehicles and baggage. British uniforms and vehicles have often been used in raids of this type.

29. To illustrate the sort of thing that can happen the following account is of value :—

"In April, 1947, a Post Office van with two men in it arrived at the gate of a Police barracks near Tel Aviv. On being asked their business the men said they had been sent for to repair the Police telephone. The guard commander got in touch with the barracks and found that the police had in fact sent for the Post Office men ; he therefore let them in without more ado. Shortly afterwards the men walked back to the gate carrying a ladder and a coil of wire. They said that the trouble was outside the compound and that they would only take a few minutes. About half an hour later there was a tremendous explosion in the barracks. Two buildings were reduced to rubble and one officer and one constable were buried by the debris and killed. The men were never seen again but it afterwards transpired that the real telephone van driver had been waylaid and his van stolen shortly before the outrage took place."

It seems unlikely that a thorough search of the van could have failed to reveal the explosive, but it should be remembered that false floors and other hollow spaces can conceal large quantities of explosive ; searchers should therefore be experienced and thorough.

Section 17.—GENERAL RULES

THESE RULES MAY SAVE YOUR LIFE—LEARN AND REMEMBER THEM

1. **Always** move about the country **with your eyes open,** and treat with suspicion any object, natural or otherwise, which appears to be out of place or artificial in its surroundings.

2. Look carefully all round a mine or booby trap **before** starting work on it.

3. It usually takes **only one man** to work on a mechanism—two is the maximum ever needed—**others keep off.**

4. Handle all mines, fuzes, mechanisms and charges **with care at all times.**

5. **Never use force.** If force is necessary for an operation, do not proceed.

6. **Never pull a slack wire and never cut a taut one.** Look at both ends of any wire before you touch it.

7. Take cover before you pull a mine or trap with a cable. Do not come out for at least 10 seconds. There may be a delay fuze.

8. If you have to leave a trap unlifted, **mark it obviously and report it.**

9. If you find any mechanism with which you are not familiar, or which you are not confident of handling, **leave it alone, mark it and report it,** so that engineers can deal with it.

PART II (RE and Infantry Assault Pioneers)

CHAPTER 4

LAYING AND RECORDING

Section 18.—PLANNING

Responsibilities

1. The responsibilities for outline planning and setting traps are laid down in Section 3, paragraphs 1 and 2. Section 1 sets out the purpose of booby trapping and gives the principles that should be observed if this purpose is to be attained. Paragraphs 1 to 3 of Section 2 indicate possible uses of booby traps in the various phases of operations.

Outline planning

2. The outline plan, which will be made by the commander in consultation with his engineer adviser, must cover the following points :—

   (*a*) What is to be done and where.

   (*b*) Who is to do it.

   (*c*) Co-ordination of the booby trap plan with the overall tactical planning, including timings of arming traps.

3. The plan will be influenced by the nature of the locality, and the time, labour and materials available, taking into account other work for which engineers and infantry pioneers are needed. It may be expected that a divisional plan will take the form of authorizing the use of booby traps in certain areas, with an indication of the type of traps (anti-personnel, anti-vehicle, delay action etc), and density required. Delegation of responsibility for detailed planning and execution in areas will usually be made to brigades, or sometimes to RE. Engineers will be placed under command or in support of the infantry, and materials and equipment will be allocated as required.

4. Once the siting has been decided upon the most important matter that requires co-ordination by the commander and staff is timing. The laying and arming of traps is work which calls for accuracy and attention to detail if it is to be fully effective ; as much time as possible should be allowed for it. On the other hand traps once laid, and particularly when armed, must be guarded so long as our troops are in the vicinity to prevent disturbance and casualties. The time between arming and evacuation of the locality should therefore be kept as short as possible. Methods of recording and reporting the locations of traps are described in Section 22.

Detailed planning

5. Once the outline plan has been made, detailed plans will follow. These will include the siting, design, construction and setting of individual traps. These tasks are the responsibility of the engineers, or when engineers are not available, infantry assault pioneer platoons.

6. The exact siting of individual traps will usually be decided upon by engineer or assault pioneer platoon officers subject to the general direction of the local commander. Whenever time permits an officer will reconnoitre the area and decide on the exact sites and types of traps to be used. He will then detail parties to these tasks and allocate the necessary equipment to them. In a hasty withdrawal, however, it may be necessary to give each setting party a number of mechanisms and tell them to make the best use of them that they can in a given area and time. Obviously the more time there is for proper reconnaissance and planning the more effective will be the use made of the available resources.

7. The principles governing the siting of traps are given in Section 1. They must be applied with due regard to the known habits of the enemy and with the utmost ingenuity. All ranks concerned in laying booby traps must make a study of the enemy's habits and must constantly be thinking out ways of surprising him. It must therefore be appreciated that throughout this chapter the methods for siting, design and setting of traps are to be taken as a guide only for use when there is no time to develop more original ideas.

8. During a withdrawal, the value of booby traps as a delaying factor must be fully exploited. Trap early and trap hard is sound policy. If the first obstacle the enemy comes to and the first house he enters is cleverly trapped so that he is badly hurt at the outset, not only will it delay him directly but it will also make him very cautious next time he comes to a similar obstacle or house. Once he has been made senistive in this way even a few branches placed across the road may be enough to check him for a few minutes while he investigates. By this means the best use can be made of a small number of mechanisms.

Design, construction and setting of traps

9. The detailed design and construction of traps is considered in Section 19, and some typical examples are given in Section 20. The procedure for setting traps is given in Section 21.

Section 19.—THE DESIGN AND CONSTRUCTION OF TRAPS

Types of traps

1. The main types of booby traps are as follows :—

   (a) Anti-personnel traps.

   (b) Anti-vehicle traps.

   (c) Delay-action charges.

   (d) Anti-lifting devices in minefields.

2. *Anti-personnel traps* are similar to anti-personnel mines. They are made of small charges of explosives operated by standard or improvised mechanisms. Some examples are given in Section 20.

3. *Anti-vehicle traps* are really improvised anti-tank mines, operated by standard or improvised pressure mechanisms, or by trip wires. They should be laid either alone or in conjunction with other obstacles on likely routes for AFVs. Anti-personnel traps may be mixed with them as anti-handling devices. Some examples are given in Section 20.

4. *Delay-action charges* may be left behind in a withdrawal or placed behind the enemy's lines in a raid. If used to destroy material they should be sited and designed in the same way as normal

demolitions (*see* Field Engineering and Mine Warfare Pamphlet No. 3*). If intended to cause casualties to personnel they should be sited in places that are likely to be occupied soon after the enemy's arrival and timed accordingly. Suitable places are dugouts, cellars and comfortable undamaged buildings. Anti-personnel traps may be laid in conjunction with delay-action charges to cause casualties to clearance parties.

5. The use of *anti-lifting devices in minefields* is described in Field Engineering and Mine Warfare Pamphlet No. 5, Part II.

The essential parts of a booby trap

6. The design and construction of a booby trap will depend upon the materials and equipment that are to hand and also on the time available. But whatever the design the following parts of a trap are essential and must be obtained or improvised :—

(*a*) A mechanism.

(*b*) A charge.

(*c*) A method of connecting the mechanism to the charge.

(*d*) A means of concealing and operating the trap, *eg*, a movable object or a trip wire.

Mechanisms

7. Standard mechanisms were described in Chapter 2. If standard mechanisms are not available improvised ones must be made. Although considerable ingenuity can be used in making improvised mechanisms they must be kept simple or they will take too long to make. Some suggested methods of employing the standard mechanisms and some improvised mechanisms are described in Section 20.

Charges

8. Charges may be made of any explosive that is to hand. Incendiary bombs or incendiary materials may also be used.

9. Charges for anti-personnel traps need not be large. Two pounds is enough but more can be used if greater effects are wanted. Stones or scrap metal can be used to produce a shrapnel effect.

10. Charges for anti-vehicle traps should be large enough to break a tank track. 20 pounds is the minimum, but 10 pounds will stop a wheeled vehicle. Section 20 describes the design of anti-vehicle traps in more detail.

11. Charges for delayed demolitions must be calculated and placed in the same way as for normal demolitions. (*See* Field Engineering and Mine Warfare Pamphlet No. 3*).

---

* Not yet published.

12. Charges for use in raids should be made up complete except for the detonator, so that the only work required on the site is to insert the detonator in the charge and remove the safety device. Such charges should be compact and capable of being carried on one man ; thus each man becomes a self-contained demolition unit. If possible the firing mechanism should be destroyed in the explosion to prevent the enemy from discovering our methods.

Standard methods of connecting a mechanism to a charge

13. Standard mechanisms are supplied with a fuze adapter which is designed to take safety or instantaneous fuze. These adapters can be seen in Figures 3, 4, 5, and 6 in Chapter 2. The snout of the adapter will fit over the fuze. The steel tongues grip the cover of the fuze and prevent it from being withdrawn accidentally. To secure the fuze a slight turn in an anti-clockwise direction is made after it is pushed home into the snout. The snout is waterproofed by means of a rubber sleeve supplied with it.

14. The fuze is led from the mechanism to a detonator which is inserted into the primer of the charge (*see* Fig 11). By using instantaneous fuze it is possible to have the mechanism and the charge some distance apart.

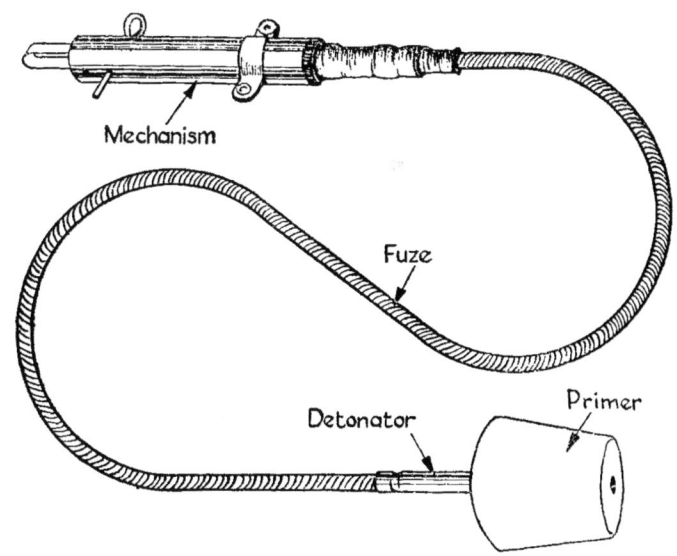

Fig 11.—Mechanism connected to a charge by instantaneous fuze

15. Detonating cord, a standard demolition accessory carried by field units, may be used instead of fuze. Although it is simpler to use fuze there are advantages in using detonating cord; it has less tendency to " whip," and its use makes possible a quick last minute connection of leads. In training, however, instantaneous fuze should be used, because it preserves the mechanisms for future use.

16. The procedure for connecting up with detonating cord is as follows (*see* Fig 12) :—

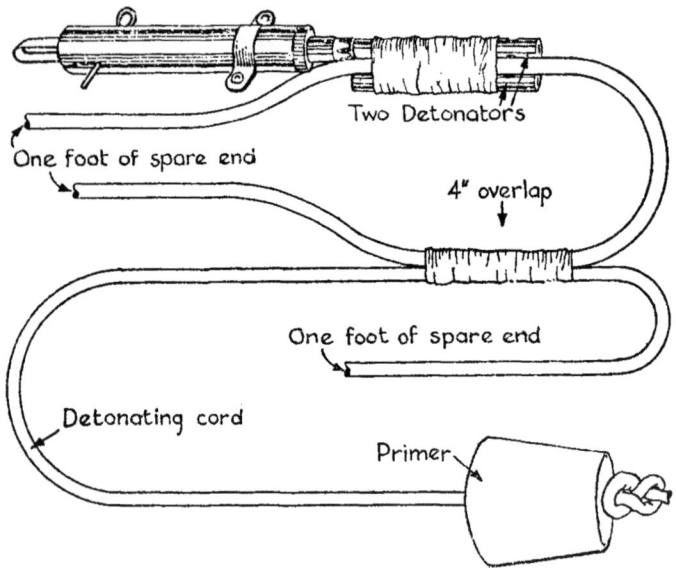

Fig 12.—Mechanism connected to a charge by detonating charge

(a) Insert a No. 27 detonator into the spring snout of the mechanism.
(b) Bind a length of detonating cord to the detonator with adhesive tape, allowing one foot of spare end.
(c) Bind another detonator to the detonating cord, on the opposite side to the first detonator.
(d) Insert a separate length of detonating cord into the primer of the charge.
(e) When the trap is ready for arming connect the two lengths of detonating cord together with adhesive tape. There should be a one inch overlap at the joint and one foot of spare end should be left on each length of the detonating cord.

Other methods of connecting mechanisms to charges

17. Electric mechanisms should be connected by electric leads to a

battery and to an electric detonator. The electric detonator is inserted into the primer of the charge in the normal way.

18. Improvised mechanisms may be fitted with a detonator and inserted directly into the primer of the charge. By this means an improvised mine can be made.

19. Whatever the method used the normal principles of initiation of explosives must be followed. These are given in Field Engineering and Mine Warfare Pamphlet No. 3*.

Section 20.—SOME TYPICAL BOOBY TRAPS

1. The first part of this section gives some examples of the ways in which the standard mechanisms may be used. The details of operation and procedures for arming and neutralizing these mechanisms have been given in Chapter 2. Section 19 explained the methods of designing charges and connecting mechanisms to charges. In the last part of this Section some improvised booby traps are described.

Switch No. 4, Pull

2. This switch must be attached to a wire. The wire may either be connected to an object that is likely to be moved, or else be set as a trip wire. Fig 13 shows a pull switch connected to an obstacle. When an attempt is made to clear the obstacle the booby trap will be sprung. Fig. 14 shows a pull switch connected to a trip wire.

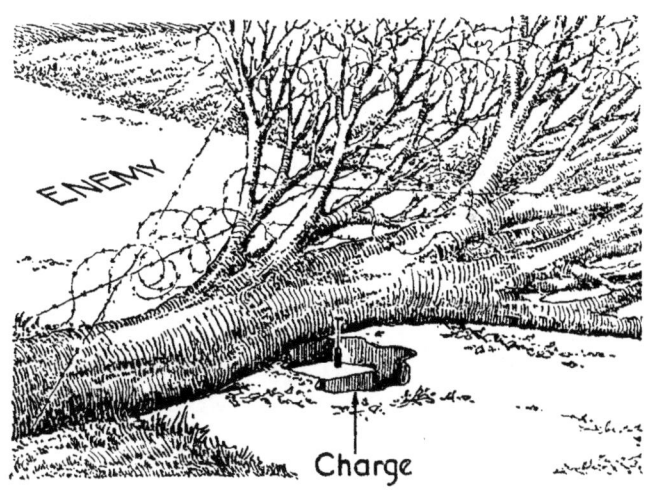

Fig 13.—Pull switch connected to an obstacle

* Not yet published.

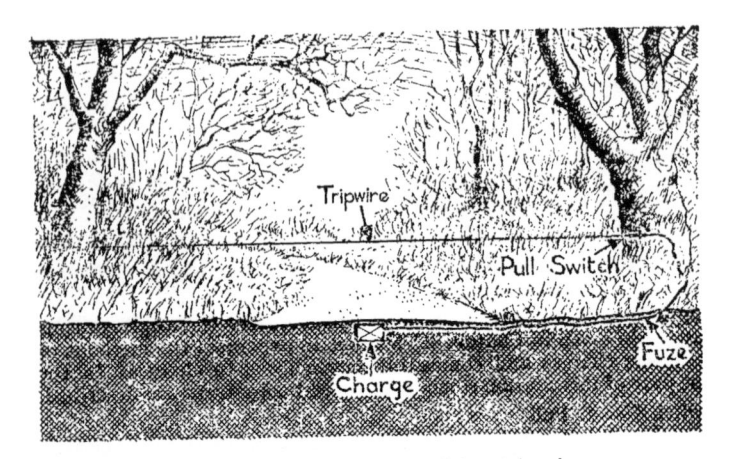

Fig 14.—Pull switch connected to a trip wire

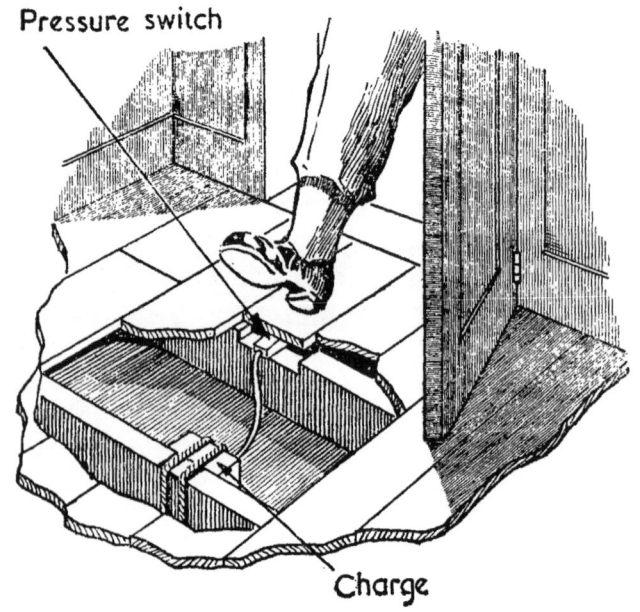

Fig 15.—Pressure switch set as an anti-personnel device

Switch No. 5, Pressure

3. This switch may be set to go off under the weight of a man or a vehicle. It can also be set under a railway line. In Fig 15 the mechanism is sited under a floorboard. A door mat can be used to aid concealment.

4. Fig 16 shows a pressure switch set under a railway line. It is important to ensure that the switch is firmly bedded on the ground so that it cannot sink with therailwhen the weight of the train comes on to it.

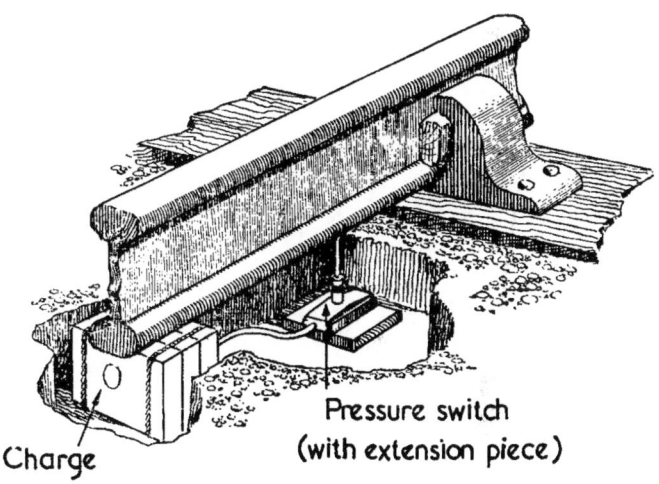

Fig 16.—Pressure switch set to operate a railway mine

Switch No. 6, Release

5. Release switches can be set under objects that are likely to be lifted, such as souvenirs or weapons, or else between objects that are likely to be moved apart. Such objects must be heavy enough (not less than 7 pounds) to prevent the release switch from going off prematurely. Fig 17 shows a release switch set under a rifle. A carpet or a piece of paper should be used to conceal the mechanism and the hole in the floor.

Fig 17.—Release switch set under a rifle

Fig 18 shows a release switch set inside a chest of drawers. A hole will have to made in the back of the chest in order to set and arm the device. The hole will be concealed if the chest of drawers is pushed against the wall.

Switch No. 9, Delay

6. The " L " Delay can be used to initiate any form of delayed demolition charge. In Fig 19 a delayed charge is set in a power station.

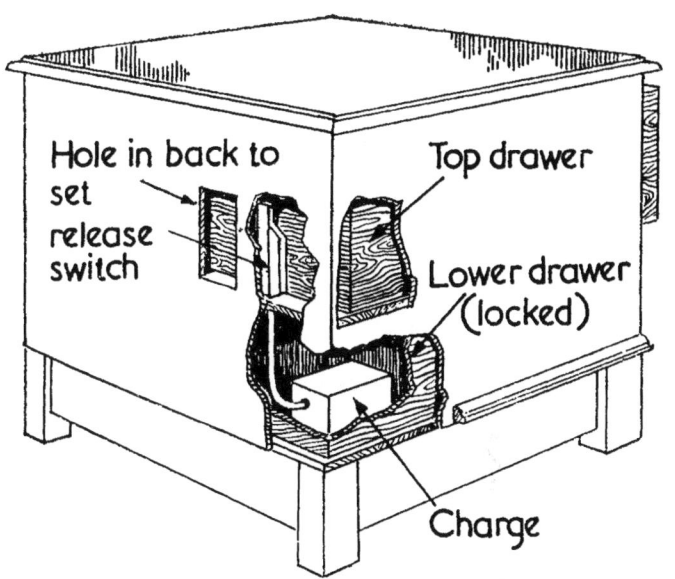

Fig 18.—Release Switch concealed in a chest of drawers

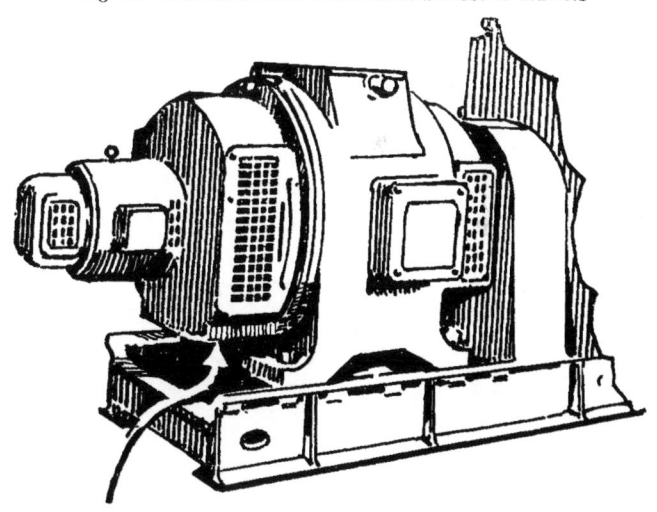

CLAM (CONCEALED)
Fig 19.—" L " Delay used in a delayed demolition

Anti-personnel mines

7. Anti-personnel mines are very suitable devices to employ on booby traps. Shrapnel mines can be used in the same way as pull switches. Anti-personnel mines, No. 5 or No. 6, can be used in the same way as pressure switches. Fig 20 shows an obstacle booby trapped with anti-personnel mines, No. 5, and shrapnel mines.

Improvised booby traps

8. If the standard mechanisms are not available improvised traps must be devised. These traps usually fall into one of the following general types :—

  (a) Direct-action anti-personnel traps, employing standard percussion igniters or grenades.

  (b) Electric contact traps.

  (c) Delay-action traps using electric contacts operated by alarm clocks, or an electrolyte solution dripping into a vessel to close the electric circuit.

  (d) Improvised anti-vehicle mines or traps.

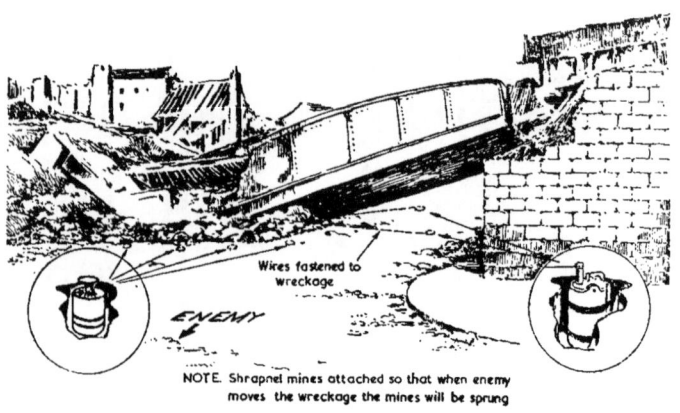

NOTE. Shrapnel mines attached so that when enemy moves the wreckage the mines will be sprung

Fig 20.—Uses of anti-personnel mines as booby traps

Direct-action anti-personnel traps

9. *Igniters, safety fuze, percussion*, which are standard demolition accessories, may be used as pull switches. The safety pin should be attached to a trip wire. When the pin is pulled out the igniter will light safety or instantaneous fuze. Once the igniter is armed in this way there is no longer any safety device, so caution is needed.

10. The simplest direct-action trap to improvise in the field is the *grenade trap* (*see* Fig 21). A short fuze must be used or the enemy will have time to take cover.

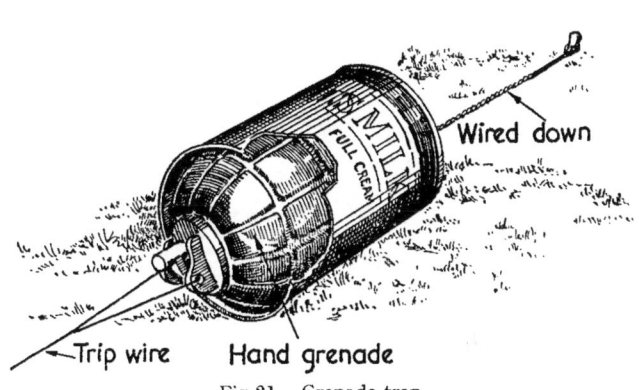

Fig 21.—Grenade trap

Electric contact traps

11. Some typical electric contact traps are shown in Figs 22 to 25 on pages 58 to 60.

CLOTHES PEG
(a)

TABLE KNIFE
(b)

To detonator

The switch will operate either by pull or release of trip wire

Trip wire in tension

Fixed contacts

METAL CONTAINER
(c)

Insulating cork

Safety pin

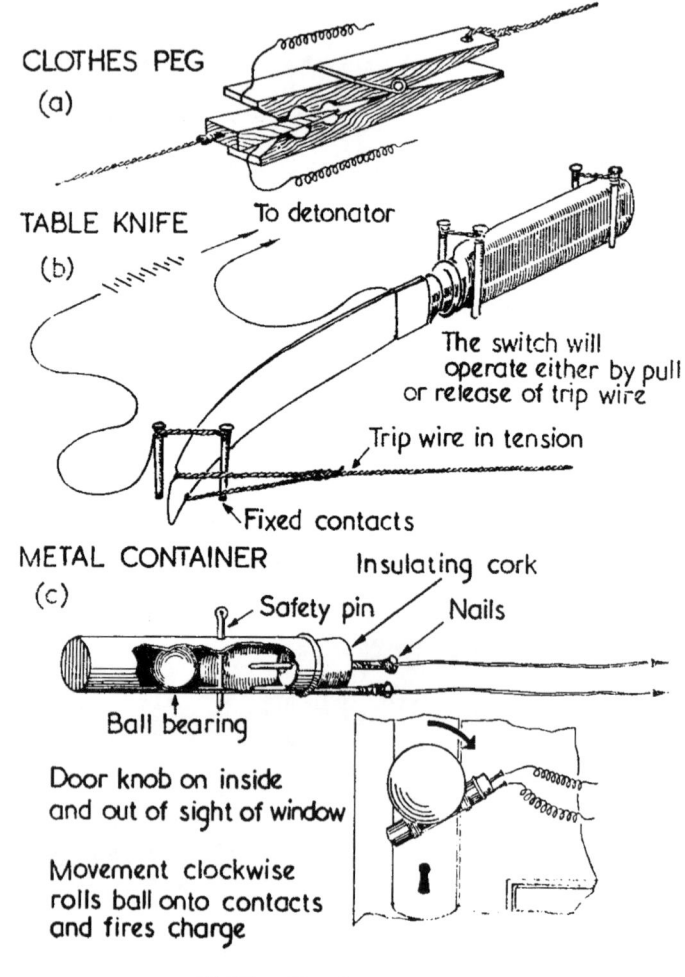

Nails

Ball bearing

Door knob on inside and out of sight of window

Movement clockwise rolls ball onto contacts and fires charge

Fig. 22.—Electric contact traps

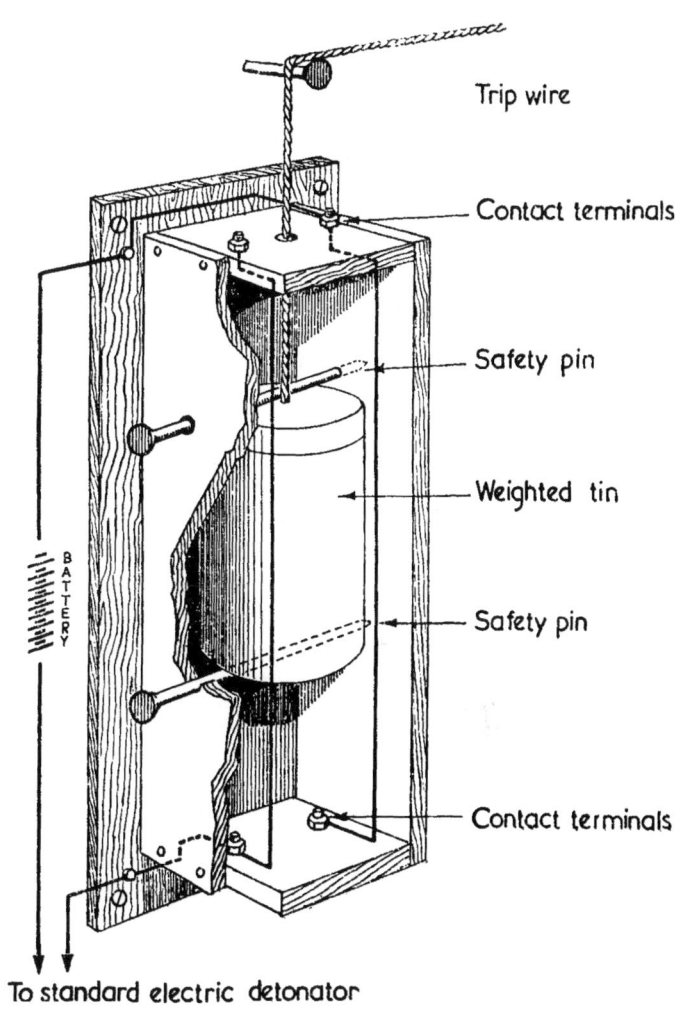

Fig 23.—Pull or Release electric contact

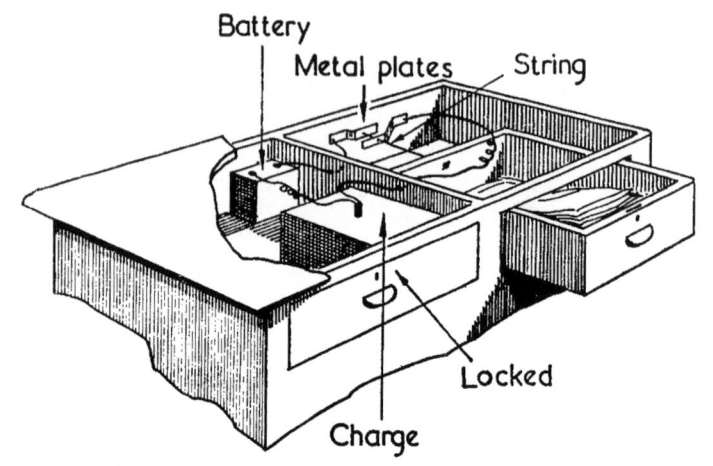

Fig 24.—Electric drawer trap (opening and closing)

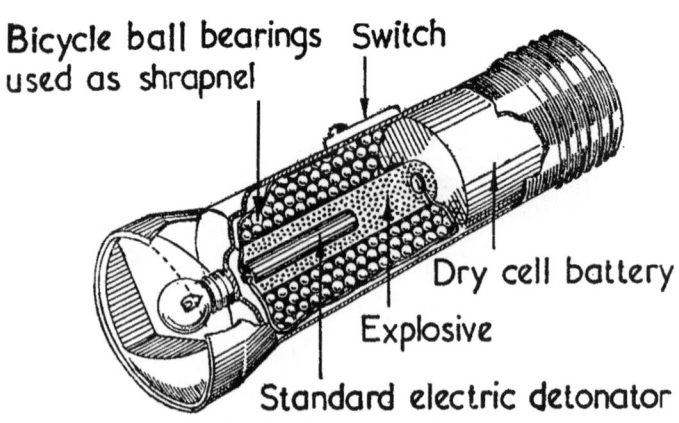

Fig 25.—Flashlight device

Delay-action traps

12. A typical electrolytic delay-action trap is illustrated in Fig 26. If the rainfall was not likely to be suitable for this device, it might instead be set in a cistern with a slow running water inlet.

Fig 26.—Electrolytic water butt

Improvised anti-vehicle mines and traps

13. If anti-tank mines are not available vehicles can be stopped with improvised mines made with pressure switches. Charges can be contained in wooden boxes and should be laid like mines so that there is a good chance of the track hitting at least one of them. Alternatively the charge can be spread across the road in a trench so that there is no chance of failure. But whatever way the charge is laid it must be arranged that at least 20 pounds of explosive is in close contact with the track.

14. If no booby trap mechanisms are available traps can be made from shells. The shells must be fitted with instantaneous percussion fuzes, and the safety devices must be removed (*see* Fig 27).

Fig 27.—Shell trap

15. Vehicles can also be stopped by charges set off by trip wires. Anti-vehicle trip wires should be made of thin stranded steel wire. The trip wire should not be attached directly to the firing mechanism because considerable tension is needed to take the sag out of the wire. Furthermore the trap might be set off by trees swaying in the wind, or by birds. Fig 28 shows a method of setting a trip wire for vehicles.

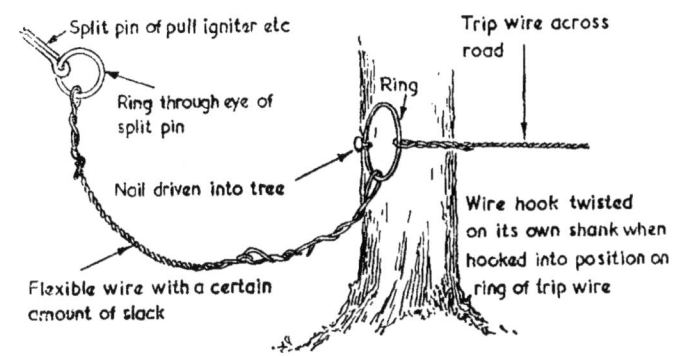

Fig 28.—Trip wire attachment for an anti-vehicle trap

The following points should be noted :—

(a) A loop or ring at the end of the trip wire is hooked over a 3-inch nail. The jerk produced by a vehicle will draw the nail. Alternatively the head can be sawn off and then the ring will slip off easily. The nail takes the normal tension in the wire.

(b) The firing mechanism can be safely connected to the ring by an unstrained loop of flexible wire and a wire hook, which is passed through the ring and twisted on itself.

(c) All wires and attachments should be strong, since a fast moving vehicle produces a considerable jerk which may snap the wires before the pull gets through to the mechanism.

Section 21.—**PROCEDURE FOR SETTING TRAPS**

1. The setting of booby traps can be a dangerous task unless it is carefully controlled. Although an exact drill cannot be laid down the following procedure is a guide ; it includes all the safety precautions that must be observed.

Inspection of mechanisms

2. Before any work begins the mechanisms must all be inspected. It is particularly important to ensure that none of them will go off prematurely when the safety device is removed.

Reconnaissance and siting

3. If a previous reconnaissance and detailed plan has not been made the commander of the party will do this as soon as he arrives on the site. He must consider the time, labour and materials he has available and decide on the exact position and design of each trap that is to be set out.

Control

4. Once the commander has been told or has decided for himself where all the traps are to go, he should set up a control point. One man should remain here in charge of all the explosives and mechanisms that are to be used. Safe routes from the control point to each trap must be detailed by the commander and should be marked out with tracing tape.

Organization of the party

5. Setting parties should be kept as small as possible. Each trap will be laid by one man or at the most two. The party should be kept dispersed as much as possible to avoid interference with one another or unnecessary casualties in case of an explosion. The commander must explain to each man exactly what he wants him to do.

Setting the traps

6. The setting men will carry out the following tasks :—

(*a*) Lay and conceal the charge.

(*b*) Fix the mechanism securely in place.

(*c*) Connect the fuze to the mechanism (*see* Section 19 paragraph 17). Do not connect the fuze to the charge. (If detonating cord is used connect a separate length to the charge, but keep the two loose ends well apart, as described in Section 19 paragraph 19).

(*d*) Conceal the mechanism and connect it to the object that is to operate it. Trip wires should always be left with some slack, as if they are set taut, premature firing may occur when the mechanisms are armed. Do not remove the safety devices.

7. Each man will report to the commander when he has done this work, but he will not leave his trap until ordered.

Inspection of traps

8. The commander will inspect the traps to see that they are properly set and concealed. He will then order the men to return to the control point by the correct route. There they will collect up the spare stores and make ready to leave the area.

Arming the traps

9. The commander will make sure that everyone is out of danger before any traps are armed. Either he or his second-in-command will then arm all the traps. A logical sequence must be followed, *eg*, in a house he should start at the top and work down.

10. Traps will normally be armed in the following way :—
 (a) Remove the safety device.
 (b) Connect the fuze and detonator to the charge. (If detonating cord is being used connect the two leads together as shown in Figure 12, page 50).

Note.—The charge is connected last so that if the mechanism is sprung when the safety device is removed there will be very little harm done. Take care when connecting up the charge that the mechanism is not disturbed.

12. There may be instances when it is safer to connect the charge first and remove the safety pin last. The commander must make this decision himself. One example of this is the " L " Delay. It is dangerous to disturb " L " Delays once the pin has been pulled out. They should therefore be connected to the charge first, and the pin should always be pulled out last (*see* Section 9).

Recording

13. The commander, or a man detailed by him, must make a record of the traps while they are being laid. He will complete this record when making his final inspection, before arming the traps. The form of these records and the manner of submitting them is given in Section 22.

Marking

14. Booby trapped sites will not normally be marked. But if our own troops are withdrawing through the area the sites should be guarded for as long as possible.

Section 22.—RECORDING

General

1. The policy for recording booby traps is the same as that for mines. This is laid down in Field Engineering and Mine Warfare Pamphlet No. 5, Part I. When booby traps are laid as anti-personnel or anti-lifting devices in minefields the procedure given in Field Engineering and Mine Warfare Pamphlet No. 5, will be followed. When they are laid alone the records will take the form given below.

Purposes of records

2. Records are required for two purposes :—
 (a) To warn our own troops who may have to use the area.
 (b) To recover the booby traps if our own troops re-occupy the area.

Types of record

3. In order to fulfil the two purposes there are two types of record :
 (a) Tactical records.
 (b) Technical records.

4. *Tactical records* are for operational purposes. They must be submitted to the brigade or higher formation headquarters as soon as the task is completed. The staff will use them to warn all troops in the area. An initial report should be sent by wireless or telephone and in this the area concerned will be described by map reference. As soon as possible a triplicate written report with sketches must be sent in by DR or LO.

5. Tactical records should include the following information :—

(a) Unit laying and authority for laying.

(b) Name and signature of officer in charge of laying.

(c) Date and time of laying.

(d) Area and buildings trapped with a sketch or trace from the largest scale map in general use.

(e) Total number of traps laid in each area or building.

(f) A special report of any delay mechanisms that are set for over 24 hours.

6. *Technical records* are for recovery purposes. The officer in charge of laying will compile as accurate a record as possible so that casualties may be avoided when traps are recovered. This record will be made out in triplicate and sent to the RE headquarters at division. In a hasty withdrawal, when it is likely that the area will be overrun immediately by the enemy, there may not always be time to make full technical records. As much detail as possible should however always be reported.

7. *Form of technical records.*—The full technical record should include all the details given in the tactical record. In addition whenever time allows it must show the details of all the traps laid. A sketch of the area will be made, on as large a scale as possible, to show the following :—

(a) The positions and numbers of traps laid.

(b) The types of traps and charges.

(c) The method of operation of each trap.

(d) Instructions for neutralization.

Separate thumb nail sketches will be made, where necessary, to explain each trap in more detail. An example of a technical record of a booby trapped area is given in Appendix E.

8. *Holding and alteration of technical records.*—The policy for the holding and alteration of technical records is exactly the same as that laid down for minefield recovery reports in Field Engineering and Mine Warfare Pamphlet No. 5. They are held by the engineers at HQs of divisions, corps and army.

APPENDIX A

Responsibilities of various arms for booby traps

All arms are divided into the same three categories as they are for mine laying and mine clearance.

	Category "A"	Category "B"	Category "C"
1. *Basic mechanisms and igniters* (Grouped by principles of operation) (a) Spring operated, ball control. (b) Spring operated control by pin or plate withdrawal.	All personnel of *all Arms*, less those in Categories "B" and "C". Recognition and a knowledge of the methods of operation of the following :— (Infantry only) British Trip Flare, Mark 1 and igniter	(a) RAC — All RAC personnel. (b) RA — fd branch any ⎫ one det per 　　　 LAA　　　 ⎬　 tp 　　　 HAA　　　 ⎭ (c) R Sigs line dets. (d) RASC One det per pl. (e) RAMC One det per fd med unit. (f) RAOC One det per fd unit. (g) REME One det per fd unit. Recognition and a knowledge of the method of operation of the following mechanisms and igniters :— German ZZ35 (Pull igniter) German DZ35 (Pressure igniter) British Trip Flare, Mark 1, and igniter British Switch No. 4, Pull, Mark 1 British Switch No. 5, Pressure, Mark 1 British Switch No. 6, Release, Mark 1 British Switch No. 9, "L", Delay, Mk. 1 German ZZ 42 Russian MUV Russian VPF	(a) All RE less Tn, Mov, Svy and Postal units. (b) Infantry Assault Pioneers Platoons. As for Category "B". As for Category "B" (*see* also FE and MW Pamphlet No. 4).
(c) Friction.		German Anz 29 N.B.—In order to obtain a full understanding of the principles of operation of mechanisms and igniters all those listed in Appendix A to FE and MW Pamphlet No.4 should be learned. Those given above are the ones most likely to be used with booby traps.	

APPENDIX A—continued

2. *Detection and clearance*	(a) Knowledge of enemy booby trap habits, places to avoid and behaviour in booby trapped areas (b) Recognition of signs used to mark booby trapped (and mined) areas (c) Use of booby trap warning signs	As for Category "A" plus:— (a) Recognition of A per devices; detection of them visually, by prodding or with mine detectors (b) Principles for clearance of buildings (c) Clearance of simple booby traps in isolated localities by *pulling*, by destruction *in situ* or, when necessary, by *hand*.	As for Category "B" plus:— (a) Reconnaissance and breaching drills for minefields which may include booby traps. (b) Clearance of all booby traps not within the capabilities of Category "B" personnel.
3. *Laying and recovery*	(Infantry only) Setting and recovery of British Infantry Trip Flares.	Setting and recovery of British Infantry Trip Flares.	(a) Setting of A per devices using standard or improvised mechanisms. (b) Methods of laying, recording, marking and recovery of A per devices in all types of minefields.

APPENDIX B

Some notes on training

Sequence of instruction

1. The table below is a guide for unit instructors in the stages that should be followed when training in booby traps. Booby trap training cannot be separated from mine warfare training, but instruction in booby traps will usually be given after basic instruction in mine warfare. *See* Field Engineering and Mine Warfare Pamphlets Nos. 4, 5 and 6.

Serial	Subject	Stages	References
1	Introduction	(a) Definition and purpose (b) Principles (c) Responsibilities	Introduction and Chapter 1 of this pamphlet.

2	Principles of mechanisms	(a) General principles
		(b) Current British mechanisms
		  (i) operation
		  (ii) arming
		  (iii) neutralization
			FE & MW No. 4. Chapter 2 and Appendix A to this pamphlet.
			Chapter 2 of this pamphlet.

3	Detection and clearance	(a) Detection (b) Neutralization (c) Procedure for searching and clearance (d) Reporting and marking	Chapter 3 of this pamphlet and FE & MW No. 6, Part II.
4	Laying and recording (for RE and Inf Aslt Pnrs only)	(a) How and where to set traps (b) Design and construction of traps (c) Uses of standard mechanisms (d) Improvised booby traps (e) Recording	Chapter 4 of this pamphlet and FE & MW pamphlets Nos 3 and 5.

Note.—In the case of RE and infantry assault pioneers it is better to teach Serial 4 before Serial 3.

General notes

2. Booby trap training must be made realistic. The following things are vital or it will be dull and of little value :—
   - (a) Suitable places for training *eg*, old houses or sheds, a minefield training area, woods.
   - (b) Plenty of working mechanisms.
   - (c) Plenty of spare caps and instantaneous fuze so that mechanisms will always make a bang when set off.

3. Once the individual stage of training is past men should be divided into teams and sent away to booby trap different areas using their own initiative. They should then be changed round and required to clear each others areas. " Casualties " should be inflicted on those who set off mechanisms carelessly.

4. Booby traps can be used on collective training. They can most easily be set by a " controlled " enemy. They must make a bang when they are sprung. There must be static umpires near them to assess casualties and explain the probable effects of the explosions. If this is not done men will become careless of the traps and will take no further interest in them.

WARNING

IT SHOULD BE EMPHASIZED IN TRAINING THAT INDISCRIMINATE USE OF BOOBY TRAPS IS LIABLE TO CAUSE MANY CASUALTIES TO OUR OWN TROOPS ; THE PLAN FOR THEIR USE MUST ALWAYS BE CO-ORDINATED BY THE GENERAL STAFF.

APPENDIX C

Scales of issue of booby trap equipment

Serial	Item	Fd Engr regt	Aslt Engr regt	Inf bn	RASC explosive lorry
	Mechanisms and initiation equipment				
1	Switch No. 4, Pull, Mark 1.	90	120	10	30
2	Switch No. 5, Pressure, Mark 1.	90	120	10	30

APPENDIX C—*continued*

3	Switch No. 6, Release, Mark 1	90	120	10	30
4	Switch No. 9, "L" Delay, Mark 1	180	240	—	60
5	Wire Trip (·032 in dia), yards	900	1200	—	300
6	Fuze instantaneous, Mark 4, feet	900	1200	—	300
7	Igniters, SF Percussion, Mark 3	720	960	200	240
8	Trip Flares (*Note* 1) ..	—	—	36	—

Marking Equipment (*Note* 2)

9	Signs, Warning, Booby trap	12	12	20	—

Notes :—

1. Trip Flares are non-lethal traps (*see* Section 3).

2. Marking equipment is an Ordnance supply, carried as unit war equipment and replaced by Ordnance.

3. Booby trap mechanisms and initiation equipment, like explosives, are an Ordnance Supply obtained through "Q" channels, and carried by the RASC.

4. Div RASC columns hold one explosive lorry for each Field Squadron. These lorries have a standard loading, part of which is shown above.

APPENDIX D

Details of packing of booby trap equipment

Serial	Item	Packing
1	Switch No. 4, Pull, Mark 1.	2 per carton 5 cartons per tin 20 tins per case (200 switches) 20-in x 9¼-in x 5¾-in, Wt 35 lb.
2	Switch No. 5, Pressure, Mark 1	2 per carton 5 cartons per tin 20 tins per case (200 switches) 26-in x 11½-in x 8¼-in, Wt 90 lb.
3	Switch No. 6, Release, Mark 1	2 per carton 5 cartons per tin 20 tins per case (200 switches) 22-in x 10½-in x 6¼-in, Wt 60 lb.
4	Switch No. 9, "L" Delay, Mark 1.	10 per tin 20 tins per wooden box (200 delays) 29½-in x 9½-in x 5¼-in, Wt 61 lb.
5	Switch (anti-lift) No. 12, Mark 1.	2 per carton 15 cartons in metal cases (30 switches) Detonator units, separately, 15 per tin.

APPENDIX D—*continued*

6	Wire Trip (·032-in dia).	25 yd coils on 3¼-in dia x ¼-in spool 400 coils in case 30-in x 22-in x 13-in, Wt 160 lb.
7	Clams.	50 per wooden box 22-in x 15½-in x 9-in, Wt 102¼ lb.
8	Limpets, Mark 3.	5 per wooden box. 14¼-in x 12½-in x 12-in Wt 62¼ lb. Bursters: 100 per metal box 8¾-in x 5¾-in x 3¼-in, Wt 3¼lb.
9	Shrapnel Mine, Mark 2.	4 per box 5-in x 9¼-in x 17-in, with detonators, Wt 54 lb.
10	Mine A Per No. 5, Mark 1.	5 mines per cardboard tube, 6 tubes, 30 fuzes, 30 pressure plates in steel box.
11	Mine A Per No. 6, Mark 1.	20 mines, with all fittings in wooden box, 21¼-in x 11-in x 8-in.
12	Trip Flares.	12 flares and 24 pickets per steel box.

APPENDIX E

Example of a technical record of a booby trapped area

Appendix "E"
Sheet 1 of 2

SECRET

RECORD OF BOOBY TRAPS
LAID IN GIESDORF VILLAGE

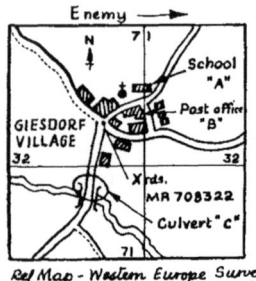

1. *Laid by* - 615 Fd Sqn RE 17(GB) Inf Div.
2. *Officer i/c laying* - Lieut R D Buggins R E.
3. *Authority for laying* - 17 (GB) Inf Div.

4. *Laid at* 1600 hrs 1 Apr 50

5. *Total number of traps laid* - 6+4 A per mines (incl 1 delay due to fire 1515 hrs 11 Apr 50.)

Ref Map - Western Europe Survey
· Scale – 1:50000
Sheet – F/1204

6. SCHOOL 'A'. 2 traps laid.

   (a) No 5 switch and 6 lb PE3 laid under third step of staircase from ground - first floor.
   (i) Operated by pressure on step
   (ii) Neutralise by removing top of step
   (b) No 6 switch laid under left hand door of wardrobe in bedroom first door on left on reaching first floor charge of 8 lb PE3 placed on top of wardrobe.
   (i) Trap operated by opening door of wardrobe.
   (ii) Trap can NOT be neutralised. Cut detonating cord at charge and fire trap.

7. POST OFFICE "B" 2 traps laid

   (a) 7 day No 9 L delay switch connected to 40 lb P.E.3 in brown trunk in cupboard under stairs ground floor. Delay due to explode 1515 hrs 11 Apr 50 ± 24 hrs.
   (b) No 6 switch on top of same box under wooden packing case marked in black "XR129" and connected through top of trunk to same charge as delay.
   (i) Operated by removal of wooden packing case
   (ii) Neutralised by lifting trunk and packing case TOGETHER as trunk has bottom removed. Then cut detonating cords at charge and fire trap - see sketch

SECRET Sheet 2

8. **CULVERT "C"**

Culvert blocked by two farm-carts wired together.
Under each cart is a 5 lb charge buried in the road.
In front of the carts are 4 x No 6 A per mines.

(i) *Operation* – 5 lb charges each operated by 1 x No 4 Pull switch connected to carts by trap wire.
   When carts are pulled **Towards** the village (North) the traps will explode.

(ii) To *neutralise* – approach from the (South) end of the culvert to avoid the A per mines, neutralise by cutting trap wires.

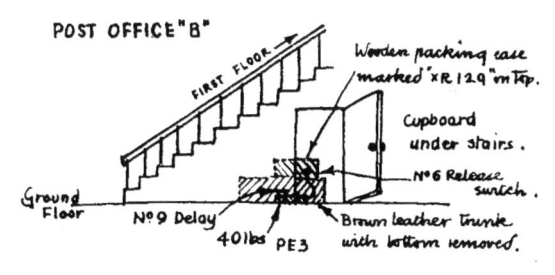

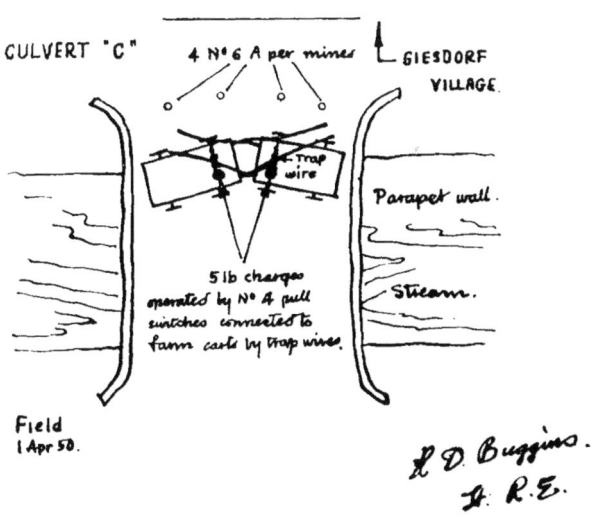

POST OFFICE "B"

- FIRST FLOOR
- Wooden packing case marked "XR 129" on Top.
- Cupboard under stairs.
- No 6 Release switch.
- Ground Floor
- No 9 Delay
- 40 lbs PE3
- Brown leather trunk with bottom removed.

CULVERT "C"

- 4 No 6 A per mines
- GIESDORF VILLAGE
- Trap wire
- Parapet wall.
- 5 lb charges operated by No 4 pull switches connected to farm carts by trap wires.
- Stream.
- Field

1 Apr 50.

L D. Buggins.
Lt. R.E.